MORE PRAISE FOR
Uncommon Measure

"Uncommon and genre-defying."
—**Alexandra Jacobs**, *New York Times*

"Incandescent."
—**Kat Chow**, *New York Times Book Review*

"Hodges considers the elemental truth pulsating beneath our experience of music and of our very lives."
—**Maria Popova**, *Marginalian*

"*Uncommon Measure* is astonishingly assured and inventive. Mixing personal reflection, reportage, literary criticism, music theory, neurology, even evolutionary studies, Natalie Hodges has pulled off something singular and wonderful. From the first page to the last, the book rides on the high wire of Hodges's virtuosic voice. It is shot through with a sinuous, luminous energy."
—**Darcy Frey**, author of *The Last Shot: City Streets, Basketball Dreams*

"There is not a sentence in Hodges's *Uncommon Measure* that does not illumine, not a single insight that doesn't lead on to a still greater one, not a moment that does not open us to wonder. In searching and visionary prose, Hodges comes close to creating a new language, one of continual questioning and delight. This is an exquisite book to be read and reread, a treasure."

—**Richard Hoffman**, author of *Half the House* and *Love & Fury*

"Hodges is a new, valuable voice in the world of music making and music writing. She moves with elegance from her own experience as a violinist to the scientific underpinnings of her subject: from math, physics, and neurology to quantum mechanics, biology, and entanglement theory. *Uncommon Measure* is a welcome debut from a wonderfully talented writer."

—**Annik LaFarge**, author of *Chasing Chopin*

UNCOMMON
MEASURE

UNCOMMON MEASURE

A Journey Through Music, Performance, and the Science of Time

NATALIE HODGES

BELLEVUE LITERARY PRESS
New York

First published in the United States in 2022
by Bellevue Literary Press, New York

For information, contact:
Bellevue Literary Press
90 Broad Street
Suite 2100
New York, NY 10004
www.blpress.org

"Untrainment" first appeared in *The Harvard Review*, Issue 55.

"The Still Point of the Turning World" first appeared in *Solstice: a Magazine of Diverse Voices*, Spring 2021.

Library of Congress Cataloging-in-Publication Data
Names: Hodges, Natalie, author.
Title: Uncommon measure : a journey through music, performance,
and the science of time / Natalie Hodges.
Description: First edition. | New York : Bellevue Literary Press, 2022.
| Includes bibliographical references.
Identifiers: LCCN 2021001707 | ISBN 9781942658979 (paperback) |
ISBN 9781942658986 (epub)
Subjects: LCSH: Music--Performance--Psychological aspects. |
Time--Psychological aspects. | Time in music. |
Improvisation (Music)--Psychological aspects. |
Hodges, Natalie. | Musicians--Psychology.
Classification: LCC ML3838 .H66 2022 | DDC 781.4/3111--dc23
LC record available at https://lccn.loc.gov/2021001707

Bellevue Literary Press would like to thank all its generous
donors—individuals and foundations—for their support.

NATIONAL ENDOWMENT for the ARTS arts.gov   This project is supported in part by an award
from the National Endowment for the Arts.

 Council on the Arts   This publication is made possible by the New York State
Council on the Arts with the support of the Office of
the Governor and the New York State Legislature.

Book design and composition by Mulberry Tree Press, Inc.

Bellevue Literary Press is committed to ecological stewardship in our
book production practices, working to reduce our impact
on the natural environment.

Manufactured in the United States of America.
First Edition
3 5 7 9 8 6 4 2
paperback ISBN: 978-1-942658-97-9
ebook ISBN: 978-1-942658-98-6

for my family

Contents

UNCOMMON
MEASURE

Prelude

If you want to change the past, all you have to do is try to record what happened in it.

In 2015, a group of Australian physicists shot a series of helium atoms through tiny slits formed by crosshatched beams of laser light.* As they watched, something incredible happened: Each of the atoms—such singular things, with their particular mass and electrical charge—seemed to ripple through not one but two parallel slits simultaneously, like waves of light or sound. In other words, the atoms managed to exist in multiple locations at the same instant, defying Newtonian laws and all classical intuition. But when the physicists placed an interferometer on the opposite sides of the slits, in order to measure the atoms' wavelike path without disrupting it, something even stranger happened: Each atom would pass through only *one* slit—exactly the way you would expect a particle to—without exhibiting any wavelike behavior at all. It was as

---

* A. G. Manning et al., "Wheeler's Delayed-Choice Gedanken Experiment with a Single Atom," *Nature Physics* 11, no. 7 (July 2015): 539–42. www.nature.com, doi:10.1038/nphys3343.

though the atoms knew *before* they passed through the slits that, an instant later, they were going to be recorded. In the words of one of the study's authors: "A future event"—the act of recording their observations—"causes the [atom] to decide its past."

One hypothesis holds that the wave represents a multiplicity of potential locations for the particle at a given moment in time, and in a given moment the particle inhabits all of those at once. Somehow, though, it is the act of recording that forces the atom to fix on a single path.

This phenomenon—which continues to pose a foundational challenge to philosophers—seems intuitively true from a human and literary perspective. Writing the book of linear time changes our reading of the past—if not the events themselves, then at least their meaning, our sense of how they happened and why. The stories that make up a single lifetime are perpetually mixed up and mixed together; our subconscious minds are constantly at work rewriting time in the margins of our memories, coaxing narrative out of chronology, temporal order out of time's chaos. In the act of recording, writing, remembering, we chart our stories onto a particular path—one way, perhaps, that from our limited human perspective we can come to terms with the infinity of past paths not taken. Writing thus distorts our sense of our own time, but it also orients us in it and helps us give it meaning.

I set out to write an exploration of music and its

relation to the science of time. Music itself *embodies* time, shaping our sense of its passage through patterns of rhythm and harmony, melody and form. We feel that embodiment whenever we witness an orchestra's collective sway and sigh to the movement of a baton, or measure a long car ride by the playlist of songs we've run through; every time we feel moved by music to dance; when we find, as we begin dancing, that we know intuitively how to take the rhythm into our bodies, that we are somehow sure of when and how the next beat will fall. Surely, I thought, there must be a scientific reason behind that innately human sense of embodied time, a way of grounding our musical intuition in physics and biology, if not completely quantifying it.

But I also wanted to write about music because it has shaped the time of my own life more than almost anything else. I have played the violin for nearly twenty years, practicing five or six hours a day for most of them, because all I wanted was to become a soloist. When I realized in my early twenties that this never would be—and never had been—a possibility for me, I began to question why I had wasted so much time on music at all. I stopped playing for a while, and though I eventually picked it up again I no longer felt the same fire or ambition. Instead I felt haunted by a monumental sense of failure, of aborted struggle and lost time. Not only had the effort and sacrifice of the past all been for naught, but the future I had planned *from* that past seemed obliterated, too.

As I wrote these chapters, however, I realized that there is no escaping the past either, no breaking out of the dance to that primeval drum. Music has inflected everything that I am *now*, in the present: my thinking about time, my relationships with my family, my sense of self. And writing about music has reminded me, too, of how much I love the violin. If all is truly said and done, if there is to be no more playing and the rest really is silence, why, then, does the past insist on returning in theme and aching variation, offering itself for memory and reinterpretation? I think of what the quantum physicist Carlo Rovelli posits in his 2017 book, *The Order of Time*: that "the mystery of time is ultimately, perhaps, more about ourselves than about the cosmos." What we all want, I suppose, is freedom from time—or at least the freedom to shape our own time at will, to change the meaning of the past from the perspective of a future present. I can't get back my old ambition and desire. Instead, I am trying to learn to love music in a different, more expansive way, one not so bound to everything I thought I wanted from it.

If you want to change the past, it seems, perhaps all you have to do is write it.

Untrainment

But all the clocks in the city
Began to whirr and chime:
"O let not Time deceive you,
You cannot conquer Time."

—W. H. Auden,
"As I Walked Out One Evening"

The pattern of my failures onstage went something like this: Days, even weeks before the performance, my brain would begin to fixate on a spot in the score that it knew I was going to mess up. It could be anything: a shift into the stratospheric reaches of the E string (the highest string on the violin); a passage of rapid-fire sixteenth notes; a finger-contorting pattern of double-stops, where you play notes on two strings at once. (Triple stops, on three strings, are even more treacherous.) It could even be—and these were the worst failures, the most painful potential desecrations—a part that wasn't technically difficult but that I really cared about musically, a central melody or a surprising harmonic change that I'd labored to shape just right. It didn't matter what it was: Once my mind had sentenced a passage to execution—or rather, to my *failure* to execute it—that

17

particular spot in the piece was done for. This was the only thing I could be sure of, going into that performance: where and when I was going to have my big botch. I'd spend the first part of the piece waiting for it, and the rest cursing myself for it.

I suppose this fixation functioned as a kind of subconscious talisman, albeit a perverse one. Perhaps if I focused hard enough on that spot and sacrificed it for the greater good of the whole piece, I'd get the mistake over with and the rest of the performance would be fine. Still, an otherwise solid performance, or even a very good one, felt sullied by those one or two spots on which my brain seemed to snag. It wasn't that I couldn't play them, or that I hadn't practiced them enough. Rather, in some subliminal way that I can't quite understand, I *needed* to mess them up.

Ego-crushing as they were, more than anything these mess-ups messed with my sense of time. Every piece of music has a time of its own, one that the musician needs to enter in order to perform it. It's a matter not only of time signature and beat, but of how you *feel* time pass within the music: Two pieces in 4/4 time may have completely different temporalities depending on the subdivisions of the beat, the flexibility of the tempo, and, above all, the music's character. Time may unfurl slowly in one and race by in another. To perform any piece, then, is to immerse yourself in its time. And when I got nervous, that's just what it was impossible for me to do. I always felt that time would stop: I'd be hurtling toward that doomed predetermined place, time whizzing by so fast in my mind that I could barely keep up with it, and then—there— with a clatter of bow and strings, it would screech to a halt. Not that I would have to stop playing, but in my mind the flow was ruined, as though the waves of sound, flowing along in their currents, had suddenly crashed against a mighty dam that they couldn't overcome. Everything afterward felt self-conscious—I couldn't get back into the time of the music because I was just thinking about how everyone was thinking about *me:* how badly I had messed up, how awkward and sorry they felt.

In the spring of my senior year in high school, for the final studio class of the last semester that I studied with my teacher, I played a piece called "La Campanella," or "The Little Bell," so named for its thematic motive of ringing, dinging high-pitched harmonics, silvery metallic tones created by stopping the string with one finger and touching it lightly with another. The piece is by Niccolò Paganini, considered by music historians to have been the first true violin virtuoso. I resent Paganini, even though he died in 1840, because it seems the man could play *anything* on the violin. Even if there weren't historical accounts of women swooning in the audience when he performed, you could tell he was a total diva by the music he wrote for himself, now bequeathed by violin teachers to generations of suffering students in the form of weekly "études." Most of Paganini's pieces are borderline impossible to play, at least if your hands are of a typical size. (It's now believed that he had Marfan syndrome, a genetic condition that distends connective tissue and can result in arms and fingers of exceptional length.) Trying to play his compositions, especially under pressure, is reminiscent of the shower scene in Hitchcock's *Psycho*—high-pitched shrieking sounds and all—where your ego is Janet Leigh and the ghost of Paganini is the shadowy figure with the knife.

In the weeks leading up to the studio class, I spent hours each day working on "La Campanella," even before getting to the rest of my practice routine. The harmonics are devilish—they flash by at lightning speed, and if you don't place your fingers exactly right the note won't speak—but nothing compares to the passage of chromatic scales and arpeggiated runs at the end, which accelerates into a blur and culminates in the resounding final chord, the bell's midnight stroke. I prepared as well as I could and by the time of the performance was able to play the piece reasonably well. No one was going to swoon, but I could get through it. Except, of course, for the passage at the end. I could play it at home, but I knew it would buckle, that *I* would buckle, under the pressure of the performance. It was only a studio class, nothing more, the audience a collection of bored students and their mostly kind, mildly competitive parents, and of course our teacher, Mr. Maurer. Even so, I tasted the sour green smack of vomit as I walked onstage.

The first part of the piece, which introduces the *campanella* theme, went fine. So did the development section, where Paganini subjects the bell to a series of relentless variations and developments, as though whacking it with a bunch of different mallets, each harder than the last. "La Campanella" is written as a rondo, a form "in which the leading theme recurs between sections and then returns to complete the composition." Rondos have the mesmerizing effect of moving you linearly and circularly through time, at the same time: By progressing from theme to theme through the development sections, the rondo consistently brings you around and back again to the music with which you began. That pattern of predictable return, that consistent cycling back, simultaneously constitutes the piece's linear progression through time. It has the effect of changing and yet not, of bringing you back to where you started and transforming that music into something both new and familiar. Indeed, after each development section, the plain, unadulterated theme rings out again, high and clarion and resolute as a clock chime, marking time with its return.

The performance was going well. Almost unbelievably well, in fact. I'd practiced counting down each time the theme returned as a way of getting through the piece, of keeping track and also keeping up morale—*only three more repetitions of the theme till the end, now two, now one.* Yet something strange started to happen as I counted those returns down. I felt—and this is the only way I know how to describe it—that I was inside the music's time, in the heart of a tolling grandfather clock whose gears turned at an allegretto grazioso rate of six eighth notes to a bar. The bell tolled on the hour of the theme, but the time in between was itself whirring and unfolding, development by development, variation by variation. Ticking off the theme's returns, I felt at the same time how each section engendered the next, how they progressed into and referred back to and complicated one another; and how, in always circling back to the theme, they shaped a globe of time, a sphere of sound. Each variation's passage changed the feeling of the theme that followed it, inflecting it with the memory of all that came before, so that even as each theme relocated itself in the present it echoed with the ghostly chimes of the past.

Then I remembered that I was supposed to mess up. I wondered, as my stomach dropped, if my teacher knew it, too—he'd heard me botch the end enough times in my lessons. I became unbearably aware of how this was my last shot, the last time he would hear me play, my last chance to prove to him that I could do it. My eyes flicked out toward the audience. Mr. Maurer was sitting off to one side in the front row as he always did, hands folded over his cardigan, face impassive.

Something about seeing him triggered that old familiar panic, and alarm bells began to sound in my brain. Time, which had been bubbling steadily along, froze. My hands seized up. Everything seemed to happen in slow motion, yet too fast for me to catch up. My left hand wouldn't shift smoothly up the fingerboard, which was unfortunate because the chromatic and arpeggiated runs accelerate from the original tempo and require, by the final measure, about three shifts per bar. My right hand, meanwhile, decided it was no longer capable of holding the bow, causing my bow hold to collapse and my fingers to lock, white-knuckled, just to keep from dropping the bow entirely. But then it happened: Just before the last chord, I dropped the bow. I was forced to play the chord by plucking the strings, in what was perhaps the world's unluckiest and most spontaneous demonstration of pizzicato.

It's (almost) comical now, but whenever I think back and try to analyze what happened, I am still stricken by the memory, sick and visceral, of how it felt when time stopped. Why is it that one's sense of time, so supple inside the music itself, seizes up and cracks beneath an audience's expectant gaze (or as soon as one becomes aware of that gaze, that expectation)? Why does getting into the flow of the music require yielding yourself to its time, feeling its flow through and around you, when all the while time is also the enemy, the thing you're running out of as you play along, trying to make it to the end and yet trying to make something of the moment while the music lasts?

If you can't get into that flow—if your nerves get the best of you and you're dragged onto the shore of self-consciousness—well, chances are you'll mess up that tricky run. Or play the last chord as an anticlimactic pizzicato and hurry off the stage with your head bowed. In performances like my botched Paganini, even when you've been dreading all the while that something will go awry—you're never prepared for it. The flow is staunched, the fabric rent; you feel punched in the gut, knocked out of the music's time and back into your own. And then, afterward, you can feel the seconds and minutes passing; you trudge through, it's all linear, you just want it to be over, you just want to make it to the end.

———

Music sculpts time. Indeed, it is a *structuring* of time, as a layered arrangement of audible temporal events. Rhythm is at the heart of that arrangement, on every scale: the cycling and patterning of repeated sound or movement and the "measured flow" that that repetition creates. The most fundamental rhythm is the beat itself, the pulse that occurs at regular intervals and thus dictates the tempo, keeps musical time. In music, a beat is no fixed thing—it can quicken into smaller intervals (accelerando) and stretch out into longer ones (decelerando), depending on the character of a given musical moment and the feeling or fancy of the performer—but it does remain periodic, predictable, inexorable. Even at the level of pitch, which is really the speed of a given sound wave's oscillation, we are really hearing the rhythmic demarcation of time, a tiny heart whirring at a beat of x cycles per second.

Yet in every piece of music there are also higher temporal structures at play. Repetition begets pattern, and pattern engenders form, at every scale; thus musical form itself constitutes a macro-rhythm, a pattern of alternations that move the listener through time. A basic chord progression, for example, revolves from the tonic (the home chord of the key signature) to the subdominant (fourth), then to the dominant (fifth), which, with its fever pitch of anticipation, propels you back to the tonic so you can start yet another progression. Similarly, in a rondo, variation and development sections perform a revolving dance around the original theme, whose returns complete the circular pattern of A-B-A-C-A. Such patterns, formal and harmonic, relate their components to one another in time. The ear can sense the harmonies to come based on the relative intensities of those that came before, or when thematic material will return by the buildup of a cadence at the end of a development section or variation. It is through this higher sense of rhythm, then, that a simple phrase or a complex form becomes a temporal object: time molded in order to manipulate emotion, putting you through the changes of the present only to bring you back to the past, locating you in a moment that is simultaneously familiar and wholly new.

I should note that I am speaking from the perspective of a musician trained only in Western tonal theory, and so I can't claim to know about the different rules and familiar tonal and formal progressions that form the backbone of other music traditions. Many cultures have their own tonalities—India's classical tuning system, for example, uses microtones that don't exist inside the Western twelve-note scale—and the way expectation is built up and subverted in and by the music is different for all of these. Yet pattern is pattern, and the music of all cultures, each with its own unique rules to be followed and broken, both weaves and rends the tapestry of audible time. Our experience of musical temporality, like our experience of the day-to-day, consists of patterns of recurrence and, sooner or later, their violation.

Yet musical time differs from the quotidian passage of ordinary time, even as it exists *within* that passage. Or, at least, it manifests how susceptible time is to our conscious perception, as much as the other way around. I suppose this is true of ordinary time, too—which flies when you're having fun and never fails to keep a watched pot from boiling—but music bends time's suppleness into sonic shape. There's more to musical time than the ticking by of a beat, just the way the perceived length of an hour is determined less by the passage of sixty minutes than by what happens to us *within* those minutes. (Who knows which is the true length?) Duration is not time—*that* is something different entirely, something utterly dependent on our perception. The first part of the Paganini seemed to take barely any time at all, so sure was I of where the music was going next . . . but an eternity unfolded within that split second when I watched my bow fall. When it is sculpted into music—tinkered into rhythms, colored by harmonic intensity, and buoyed or burdened by human emotion—time somehow becomes plastic and malleable, expandable and contractible. There's a term for that interplay of stretch and compression: *rubato*, literally the "robbing of time." The malleability of our perception of time is the stuff of music itself. The concept of passage, the way we generally conceptualize time—seconds elapse into minutes, today becomes tomorrow—is of getting through from one thing to another. In music, time is inseparable from sound itself. A piece of music is a multidimensional entity, a creation molded from time's clay.

Thus moments of musical time are connected, in our minds, by our uncanny predictive sense of when the next beat will fall, of what the next chord could be. But what is that sense, exactly? Turns out there's a word for it, and neurological research behind it: *entrainment*, the ability to synchronize the body's movements with a beat, "a perceived periodic pulse that listeners use to guide their movements and performers use to coordinate their actions." Aniruddh D. Patel, a leading researcher in music cognition at Tufts University and a 2018–2019 fellow at Harvard's Radcliffe Institute for Advanced Study, believes the key to entrainment lies in the brain's capacity for anticipation. California sea lions and Asian elephants can also entrain to a beat, he told me, as well as several species of parrot. Still, it is the human brain, with its ability to entrain to a beat and then turn it into something more—a lullaby, a victory march, a sick jazz groove—that, for him, holds the most interest and importance. "Every human culture," Patel writes, "has some form of music with a beat: a perceived periodic pulse that structures the perception of musical rhythm and which serves as a framework for synchronized movement to music." In other words, humans don't just *hear* beats—we *feel* beats, internalizing them in our bodies and using our bodies to express their time. Even monkeys have a difficult time learning to tap in sync with a metronome, "a task which is trivially easy for humans, even for those with no musical training."

Patel has consolidated his research on human entrainment into a theory of beat perception called ASAP: Action Stimulation for Auditory Prediction.

When I met with Patel, a soft-spoken man with a low voice and kind eyes, at the Radcliffe Institute on a bright afternoon in October 2018, he explained his theory's central proposition: that movement itself is inseparable from beat perception, and that it indeed "plays a causal role" in entrainment. The human brain has an especially streamlined loop between its auditory and motor-planning regions, called the dorsal auditory stream. That circuitry both enables the brain to predict when the next beat will occur and coordinates how the body will move in response: a moving bow, a vibrating finger, a bobbing head, a tapping foot. When the auditory cortex, located in the temporal lobe near the center of each of the brain's hemispheres, picks up a recurring pulse, it fires an ongoing stream of action potentials, or neural signals, to the cortexes responsible for motor planning, conveying how far apart each beat falls from another. But once those first preliminary signals are received, the motor cortex starts firing back its own electrical impulses, helping the auditory regions refine their own predictive sense of when the next beat will fall and creating an ongoing loop of action potentials. In other words, our motor coordination affects our ability to keep in time as much as our *sense* of time affects our motor coordination. Rhythm engenders movement, and movement in turn becomes rhythm.

Entrainment, then—the syncing to, and bodily expression of, a particular beat—enables both performer and listener to stay in the flow of musical time. And entrainment operates at levels higher and more metaphysical than the perception of the physical beat alone. The next beat isn't the only thing the performer has to think about, or to which the listener responds: Both also have to tap into the higher rhythms of phrase structure and the piece's form. What pattern of harmonies constitutes the theme? And when does the theme recur, either in its resounding entirety or, in the development sections, in ghostly snatches of its former self? It is through entrainment at all temporal levels that music allows us to break out of the quotidian rhythms of day-to-day time—our routine alternations between anxiety and boredom, thought and action—and thus to break out of ourselves.

For the listener, this transcendent groove is easy enough to fall into upon even a first listening, at least if the piece retains some shadow of tonal and structural tradition. (Think of how in a pop song, even one you've never heard before, you know instinctively when the chorus is coming up.) A more encompassing kind of anticipation is demanded of the performer, however. It requires a deep knowledge of every element of the score, and only comes with intense and relentless practice over time—and yet it can, at least in my experience, be shattered by that first quickening of one's own terrified pulse onstage. Knowing what's to come—and, more importantly, feeling secure in that knowledge—allows you to let go and focus intensely on communicating, on keeping the piece's time and yet making its expression feel spontaneous. But when all you can fixate on is your weird psychotic certainty that you're going to mess up, no matter how well you've prepared—that obliterates your sense of *being in time*. That dread weighs everything else down, so all the parts that might have redeemed the mess-up are wasted. When I am nervous, it feels like a five-pound weight has been added to my bow; my left hand seizes up and grips the neck of the violin in a kind of chokehold. Every moment feels burdened. And no wonder—I can't focus on making a moment of the music when I am panicking that two bars on I am going to have a memory slip, or that my fingers will tangle up in the development section's fast passages. Nothing flows, yet somehow the phrases pass me by; I can't make them lead and lean into one another the way I've practiced at home; I can't rob the time or give it back. I play the music in tempo but cannot feel it *in time*.

I wondered if that strange connection between nerves, entrainment, and temporality might have its roots in Patel's ASAP theory, with his insight that "the motor system plays a causal role in beat perception." Performance anxiety has been shown to profoundly affect the motor-planning regions of the brain, the same cortexes responsible for coordinating the body's response to a beat in ASAP. A 2015 study in *Nature* by the cognitive and behavioral scientist Michiko Yoshie measured "focal reductions in activity" in the brain's motor-control regions when subjects were asked to perform even trivial fine-motor tasks in front of an audience. If the motor system is responsible for entrainment, and performance anxiety messes with the motor system, then shouldn't performance anxiety inhibit entrainment also? According to Patel, yes, it's possible. "Specifically, ASAP predicts that the disruption of normal activity in motor planning regions will impair beat perception"—and it is the motor-planning regions of the brain that are affected by performance anxiety. Another of Yoshie's studies measured the impact on pianists when they had to perform under scrutiny: "persistent low-level muscle tension in the arm and shoulder, induced by the presence of an audience, [led] to increased keystroke force resulting in a loss of fine control of dynamics and temporal fluency within musical performances." The performers' nerves, in other words, disrupted the feeling of the music as a natural flow in time, both for them and for the listeners.

"Persistent low-level muscle tension" sounds about right. Even though you can still execute the basics—move the bow, finger the notes—it's the nuance of the performance, the "temporal fluency" and spontaneity of expression, that often gets lost. Once, quaking backstage before a performance of a Beethoven string quartet with an infamously difficult first violin part, I felt my left arm go numb, then my right. It was my first chamber music performance in college; on my way to the concert hall, I had stopped to hyperventilate into the paper bag that had held my lunch. Backstage, Gordon, our second violinist, remarked that his arms had been feeling numb and tingly all day. "I'm probably going to mess up because of it," he groaned, rolling his eyes. Well, now that messing up was on the table, *someone* had to do it. (Who knew muscle tension was so contagious?) In the performance, Gordon was fine. Guess who wasn't.

A friend who used to stammer once told me that he "always thought it had something to do with time." I was telling him about the pianist study, how performing under pressure affected the players' sense of time's flow, and he nodded with deep recognition. "I think it's the same with words. If I had to speak, I dunno, in front of a group or something, and if I thought of what I wanted to say in the moment and could say it right then, I'd be fine. But if I had to wait to speak, and keep the words in my mind and then force them out . . . It was like time had stopped. I just couldn't speak."

I know how he feels. In many ways, my mess-ups were like musical stammers. Indeed, Patel posits that the heightened connections between the brain's auditory and premotor regions evolved partly because they facilitated vocal learning and speech in early humans, enabling our ancestors to "mimic a wide range of sounds" (requiring motor control of the mouth, throat, lungs, vocal cords, et cetera), and eventually *use* those sounds to express themselves and communicate with others. Speech—which, like music, connects sounds in time to express emotion and create meaning—has its own performed element, predictive yet improvisatory: You think as you speak, your words have to keep up with your thoughts in time. It's a stunning capability, automatic and instinctive and miraculous. And yet it can shut down the instant you start thinking too hard about the act of speaking itself. You open your mouth, but the words won't come; you're trying to tell your story, but the story gets lost amid the self-conscious strain of the telling.

The same goes for musical performance, at least for me. No matter how well I know the music, the certainty that I will mess up checkmates any musical conviction I have, even about a piece I know inside and out. It doesn't always happen; but when it does, there is nothing I can do to stop it. My self-doubt begins to creep along the periphery of my consciousness, clouding my vision of how I want to play. It's as though my mind has to toggle between two time signatures, that of my ego and that of the music. The two run along fundamentally different grains, like cross-rhythms, where triple meter fights against double. One is a self-absorbed, interior time—the time of thought and of self-consciousness, of the individual mind navigating its way through the world—while the other contains the possibility for a kind of communal time, in which the self can be in sync with others. The music wants to flow, but my ego wants to stop all the clocks: As much as it demands to be the center of attention, it flies into a panic at the thought of everyone looking at it, a frightened demon-child that doesn't know what it wants yet clamors to have its way.

In a perverse way, then, doesn't the ego preserve a role for itself by undermining itself, by making sure it messes up? Performance embodies the paradox of losing yourself and yet asserting yourself, the way an actor takes the stage in order to become someone else entirely (or, perhaps, how he becomes someone else entirely in order to take the stage). In music, you have to suspend your ego, arrest the rhythms of its constant self-conscious chatter and cede them to the music's time—although of course it is the ego that is performing, that is indeed crucial to the idea of performance itself. You have to relinquish all thought of who's looking at you, of how hard you've worked, even of how well you want the performance to go, in order to become the music, immerse yourself fully in the music's time. You have to take yourself out of one time in order to fully command the next.

Why is that so hard? Maybe it's because as a performer, you don't produce something concrete: You have to keep remaking whatever it is—the routine, the layup, the dance, the music—in time, each time. What was good or even perfect in practice is irrelevant, because all that matters is what happens now, in this moment, when the lights are bearing down and the hall has gone quiet and the audience has concentrated its expectant energy on you, there, now, alone. Performance anxiety is, in part, the anxiety of re-creation, inherent in any temporal art (or sport, for that matter); and for me the anxiety of re-creation is the fear of losing what I once had. It's the tension between two (seeming) inevitabilities: the comfort of the score, what you *know* you know how to do because you've practiced it a million times, and the dread certainty that you are going to mess up because, well, you have to, because that's just what you do. At its heart, I think my chronic performance anxiety was nothing more or less than my fear of relinquishing control over the moment, my desperation to assert that my performance—not to mention all the work leading up to it—*mattered.* If I hadn't spent so many hours in the practice room attending to every little articulation and agonizing over the direction of each phrase, I don't think I could have convinced myself that the stakes were so high. How was I going to prove to myself and everyone else how much I cared, how hard I had worked, when I had only one shot to get it right? The certainty that I had set myself an impossible task would make me tense up—and that's when perfection was more likely to slip through my fingers.

Mr. Maurer, my high school teacher, having

watched me struggle, once told me to try to create a kind of blankness in my mind, a warm sunlit calm where you feel far away from everyone and everything as you play. "It's like going fishing," he said, and though I think I understand what he meant I've never been able to get there. It doesn't address the psychological root of the problem, or at least of *my* problem. It seems, to me, like trying to make your mind go blank during meditation, and then all you can think about is not thinking, which itself is a thought and so makes you a failure. The thought I've never been able to get past, the thought that trips me up every time, is: *Just because you did this before doesn't mean you'll be able to do it now, in front of all of them.* My pulse quickens, I feel their eyes boring into my head—and then time stops. I'm done for, wrenched out of the flow, snagged on the hook of their seeming expectation and my fear that I'll fall short.

It *is* like going fishing, but here I am at once the fisherman and the desperate fish, gasping and wide-eyed, drowning in the air.

—

I was packing up after the Beethoven concert when Ying, my college violin teacher, came up to me. She and Mr. Maurer are as different as it is possible to be, both in teaching style and general aesthetic: She is in her thirties, wears long sparkly earrings and embroidered jackets, hikes the Alps in her spare time, and practices a particularly punishing form of spiritual yoga. I hadn't been studying with her long, only a few months by then, but she was already indoctrinating me in a school of violin playing of her own invention, whose vocabulary sounds like something out of a psychedelic Pilates session: "Lengthen your spine as though it is a taut string of pearls"; "Feel the energy shooting out from your fingertips"; "Imagine you are a tall tree with roots." (Mr. Maurer, a child prodigy who is now in his seventies and hails from an older-school tradition of playing, taught by more direct commands: "More bow"; "Please vibrate"; "Play with a bigger tone"; "Remember, the tempo *is* the character.") Ying was more like a cool older sister than a teacher only, and she encouraged me both to experiment and to relax. Playing for her in our lessons made me feel free.

"Are you okay, Natalie?" she asked searchingly. "There was something about your energy—I thought maybe your wrist was hurting again."

I told her I almost *wished* it had been my wrist— the phantom of a ligament hyperextension in eighth grade, caused by overpracticing, that still plagues me off and on—not some stupid psychosomatic tense-up caused by stage fright.

"I see," Ying said. "But you played very well, even so. You kept going; you didn't have to stop."

"I could have played so much better."

Ying shook her head and smiled at me. "Think about how extraordinarily the four of you moved as a group. The others were helping you—didn't you feel it? You were so in sync. They were sending you their energy. They were with you the *whole time*."

She was right—we hadn't had to stop. Time had kept on flowing. The performance had been fearful but fine, with only a few noticeable slips here and there. And it was because of them, the other three players, Audrey and Gordon and Martine, that I'd been able to keep going. I realized then how sensitively they had played: how Audrey had played *toward* me, buoying my sound with her cello's bass line; how Gordon and Martine, the second violinist and violist, had sent me the steady energy of their eighth-note accompaniment during my runs, staying in time with me no matter what, grounding me and giving me something to hold on to. During the performance, they had endeavored to entrain themselves to the patterns of not only their own parts but mine, too, to anticipate what help I would need and preemptively provide it. On my way home I burst into tears, overwhelmed with gratitude and a sadness I couldn't quite name.

Music, evolutionarily, has always been about entraining minds. A 2015 study of "statistical universals" of human music, led by musicologist Patrick Savage and published in the *Proceedings of the National Academy of Sciences*, posits that the ability to make and appreciate music offered our ancestors more than just what Steven Pinker has called "auditory cheesecake": a real biological advantage that increased their chances of survival. The uncanny ability to entrain one's own body to a beat translates into the equally uncanny ability to sync one's movement with the movement of others. The study suggests that a cross-cultural or "universal" purpose of music was to synchronize group actions, because a bonded, cooperative group—on the hunt or on the move, learning to fight and gather and build in tandem—was more likely to outcompete a discombobulated one.

But there is another reason, I think, that musicality—this mysterious human capability, seemingly so superfluous to our survival—evolved in our ancestors and has stuck around since. The desire to make music is as much a desire to assert the individual self as to connect with others. Otherwise there would be no soloists, no Paganini, no one willing to take the risk of performing Paganini's music.

Why, then, does the ego get in the way of its own longing for expression? On one hand, it is inherently egotistical—presumptuous, even—to get up onstage and demand that others listen to what you have to say. But at the same time, performing requires humility: a willingness to risk being humiliated or misunderstood, and to lay yourself bare so you can try to say what you mean (and what you think the composer meant). *That* is what is at stake in performance: nothing more or less than the longing for self-expression, to connect with others and be heard by them. Perhaps the dorsal stream evolved in order to meet our need, at once egotistical and vulnerable, to try to make ourselves known to one another.

The obvious solution to my anxiety, of course, would be to stop performing: to practice whatever and whenever suits my fancy, to play for fun, to play for just myself. And yet I cannot. As soon as I walk onstage, I usually wish I were anywhere else in the world—but whenever someone asks me if I want to perform? I jump at the opportunity, saying, *yes, I do, I would love to play*. And I mean it. I can't get away from it; I keep sailing into those dire straits, somehow. It's not that I have anything in particular to say with my music. It's just that even so—even when something goes awry, and I am lying gutted on the floor of my room afterward, my violin case shoved into the corner—I still want to be heard, still want to speak.

"Don't try your best," Ying told me once, on a bright April morning in my junior year as an undergrad. It was my last lesson with her. She was going to move away to London in the summer, where she said she feels more at home. She would go in June, taking her bright energy and her embroidered coats with her. Her two other students and I had planned a going-away recital and reception for her, during which each of us would play a full sonata. I was to play Bach's Sonata in C Major for solo violin, which she and I worked on, off and on, for pretty much the entire time I had been her student. The second movement is a devilishly tricky fugue, a labyrinth of repeated micro-themes that pursue one another in a seemingly endless four-voice canon, a microscopic rondo in every measure.

Ying's advice took me aback. It would be the last time I'd play for her for who knew how long, and I was damn well going to try my best. I told her so, and she laughed. "Just this once. Try it and see if it helps you not get so nervous." I thought of the *Nature* study—whose participants applied *more* force, tried harder at the task, when they thought they were being judged—and reluctantly agreed.

On the night of the performance, my body put me through the usual sequence of reminders that it doesn't like going onstage: need to hyperventilate, multiple trips to the bathroom, compulsion to vomit, compulsion to eat everything in sight. The one thing that kept me going was the knowledge that Ying would be in the audience. I wanted her to know that I was grateful for everything she had done for me, that I would keep working hard at what she had taught me, that I hoped she'd come back one day.

I didn't want her to go; I wanted to seize that moment and make it last.

Some people get to experience a timeless,

out-of-body, Nike-ad moment of transcendence when they perform, in which they relinquish their anxiety and forget the audience and trust their preparation and Just Do It. I imagine such moments to be like a globe of time, blown glass expanding. . . . But the shattering reality is that, for me, it has never happened that way.

What I *did* experience that night, however, was the feeling of being acutely *in* body and *in* time. I took all of Ying's psychedelic Pilates hocus-pocus and believed in it as mightily as I could. This was the last time I would get to play for her, and I didn't want to lose any moment of it to the blinding force of fear. I grounded my feet on the floor, pretended she was the only one in the audience, focused all my energy toward her, and played for her alone. I didn't need to worry about what she was thinking; I knew she wouldn't judge, no matter what happened; I just wanted to tell her, to *show* her, in some way, what being her student had meant to me. My first notes halted, faltered a little—but as I pushed on and gathered my breath, I began to experience a unity of body and mind that I had never felt before. I felt them working together in a rhythmic tandem, caudal auditory regions and inferior parietal cortex preparing the body for what would come next, muscle memory dragging my thoughts back from the precipice when they veered too close to self-doubt. Mind and body kept each other in time. Time didn't dissolve in a triumphal moment of transcendence, but neither did it come to a halt because I'd seized up. Instead, I felt myself moving along with it. During that performance I was acutely aware of my body—my feet like tree roots in the floor, the energy and the sweat on my fingertips, the pearls of my spine—and also of time; but not time as the ticking by of moments only, or as passage only, but as an entirety, a whole moment made up of little moments connected seamlessly to one another. The sonata contained, somehow, those three years of work with Ying, of marching forward and doubling back, of halting progress and hopeful return. In the thirty minutes of the music's unfolding, I saw the time I had spent with her take form: a rondo, a shape of time, a sphere suspended in the dark continuum of memory, an entity that held. Every moment was constantly being added to the next; neither past nor future existed, only a continuous present. I had this time, it belonged to me, it always would. And there, in the audience, was my teacher. For now, that was enough.

Now, when I'm nervous but determined not to try my best, I pick out one person in the audience and play for them alone, concentrate my energy toward them with all my might. In playing for that person, I am taken momentarily out of myself: My mind forgets to go blank; my muscles forget to freeze. Usually I can't see the person well: They are a face in a crowd, a dark shape in a dim room. But it is their presence that matters, that grounds me in this moment and this place. I cast my line, feel their attention catch; try to stay calm as together we are set adrift into the stream of the music's time.

A Sixth Sense
Notes on Improvisation

*And the earth was without form, and void;
and darkness was upon the face of the deep.*

—Genesis 1:2

The pianist moved back and forth across the keys, her hands like two birds lilting and alighting, her hair a dark pendulum. The song was a song from the past, and everyone in the audience seemed to know how it went. They sang it with her in the beginning. But then new lines began to split off from the main body of the theme, like the branches of a tree; strange harmonies suddenly flowered forth; the time signature shifted from a bright two-step to a shadowy waltz, like leaves turning in the light. As each transmutation of the theme grew organically into the next, one got the feeling that their order had to have been predestined from the very start, so shot through was the sound with a luminous inevitability, each variation like and yet unlike the original melody, *of* it and yet wholly other. Even now, though, I don't know that I can describe to you, really, what it was like, because all of these changes—these variations and variegations and the sum they added up to, their unified whole, this tree of time—*this music* didn't exist until the moment the pianist performed it, and, apart from the concert recording that's now on YouTube,* it never will again.

The piece was an improvisation on the German folk song "Ein Vogel wollte Hochzeit machen," the place and time was Ruhr, Germany, 2009, and the pianist was Gabriela Montero, the Venezuelan artist and activist known for her spontaneous, classical-style improvisations in concert—that is to say, her performances which are really acts of composition, unfolding in real time. She may be best known to the American public for performing alongside Anthony McGill, Itzhak Perlman, and Yo-Yo Ma at the inauguration of President Obama in 2009, but her career has spanned appearances in recital halls and with orchestras across the world, including the New York Philharmonic, the Los Angeles Philharmonic at the Hollywood Bowl, and the Warsaw Philharmonic, as a winner of the 13th International Chopin Competition in 1995. Her

---

* Steffen Hermann and Maria Stodtmeier, "Gabriela Montero—Improvisations, Brahms & Ginastera (Full Performance)." YouTube, uploaded by Nene, June 13, 2017, www.youtube.com/watch?v=fkXG-2LukrE.

performance in Ruhr, part of the region's annual piano music festival, followed what has become the formula for her concerts worldwide—if, that is, it can really be called a formula at all. After Montero has performed a few pieces from the classical canon—a Rachmaninoff concerto, for example, or a Ravel fantasy—members of the audience will offer melodies for her to improvise upon, usually by standing up and singing them to her across the crowd. Montero smiles; she takes every volunteer seriously (if a person's singing elicits a titter, she asks the audience, almost indignantly, "Why are you laughing?"). Then she looks up at some far-off place beyond the ceiling, fingers a few ghostly notes along the keys, and launches into the beginning of a piece whose every note is as yet unknown.

There's a certain strangeness to watching the video of this concert over and over again, as I have, more times than I can count. After all, the music was supposed to exist only once in time, and then never again; here, pressing the REPLAY button is really a way of commanding "re-create." Indeed, the fact of the recording itself seems fundamentally at odds with the point of her performance, at least as Montero describes it. "What's beautiful about improvisation is that it's really something very spontaneous, and that it never happens again," she says in the video's accompanying interview. "And I think in this world where so many things are repeated, and so many things are predictable and calculated, it's nice to do things that are happening just once, very free, and that's it. You know?"

It's that idea of freedom, that *association* of freedom with impermanence, that makes Montero's performances unique within the classical concert circuit. Indeed, unlike jazz improvisers, Montero is tapping into a type of performance not commonly associated with classical music in the first place. One of classical music's traditionally defining features, as a genre and a practice, is its emphasis on committing things to memory, then resurrecting them *from* memory through repetition. This plays out, in one way or another, at every stage of the process by which music is brought to life. Composers preserve their ideas through meticulously notated scores that dictate how the piece is to be re-created in the concert hall—not only the notes but the tone, articulation, dynamics, and character with which those notes are to be played. These scores are then analyzed and often memorized by musicians in rehearsal, who practice until the music and its motions become a new fact of their bodies, taking possession of the muscles, some cocktail of the composer's commands and their own interpretations entering the bloodstream like an IV drip. Beyond even this, though, is the notion of classical music, like any canon, as a living past, one that can be resurrected and imported from one time into another, so that Beethoven lives again with every performance of his Ninth Symphony, Bach with every piano student who opens his *Well-Tempered Clavier.* It is the responsibility of musicians to keep that past alive, through performances that inevitably become acts of memorialization. Thus not only the music itself, but the traditions of how to play it, are passed down and down again through the fires of time until they have been forged and polished into a ring of gold, a goliath and immovable canon.

I came across Montero's playing in September 2019, shortly after performing a concert with a friend from high school and his professional indie rock band. Jake and I had played together in the past, usually on songs of his own creation; he'd write the melody and lyrics and then bring different instrumentalists into his studio to record to a click track, making up whatever sounded good in the moment. He is a consummate improviser, and was always encouraging me to try: "Just relax! Just have fun! It doesn't matter if you mess up." I would always refuse and insist on writing out my own scores, shaking my head and saying, "How am I supposed to know what comes *next*?" Jake would laugh and say, with a twinkle in his eye, "You don't—that's why it's fun." But I spent so much time telling him I couldn't improvise that eventually he believed it. When I played with him in September, I felt both grateful and a little crestfallen, somehow, when he presented me with charts he had written out himself. "I thought you'd feel more comfortable having this," he said, beaming, and even though I *was* more comfortable I couldn't help but feel like I was missing out, diligently reading my sheet music (to which I ended up adding neatly penciled fingerings, bowings, and dynamic markings out of habit) while everyone else improvised their hearts out onstage.

I am not alone in my inability to improvise, of course. Unlike my friend, who has been jamming on the piano and guitar since our elementary school days, most classical violinists don't grow up learning to improvise; we are focused on learning to read music, then on learning pieces from scores, then, finally, on memorizing them. When you're indoctrinated in that method of learning for long enough, improvisation comes to seem antithetical to the kind of hard work and discipline necessary to make "real" music—though nothing could be further from the truth, and such a mind-set is laced with traces of the elitism and racism that historically have made classical music turn up its nose at rock, hip-hop, and jazz. This attitude has also affected the careers of improvisational artists like Montero, who, no matter the extent of their classical training or the formidability of their programming, have had to struggle to be seen as "real" classical musicians. Within a style and school so focused on prophylactic discipline and rigor, on anticipating and preparing for any possible thing that could go awry, improvisation seems fundamentally out of place, nonsensical even. While classical music is about repeating, analyzing, controlling, and re-creating, improvisation necessitates a kind of surrender to time itself. For Montero, this is what makes improvisation so natural; it was her way of "telling stories" as a child in Venezuela, of narrating what her days were like, what she saw around her, how she felt at a particular moment. Sometimes she would talk as she played along, narrating her improvisations: "So I would say, 'And now my father wakes up, and this is what my father sounds like. And now my father goes out and comes back in a bad mood, and this is what my father sounds like.'"

But her talents as an improviser—though encouraged by her childhood piano teacher—were quashed, during her adolescence, by a teacher who told her that improvisation wasn't worthy of performance and shamed her into stopping. Now, much of the resistance she faces stems from skepticism as to whether it is actually possible to do what she can do at all. One of the more common accusations among her detractors, according to Montero, is that she plants people in the audience to sing preprepared themes and travels with them on her tours. They're wrong, but for them it seems the only logical explanation. Montero's improvisations are as complex in form as any fugue, as expansive and wide-ranging as any concerto . . . and yet they are developed at a moment's thought. It should be impossible to do what she does, to pluck so much sound out of so much silence, to generate form so effortlessly and instantaneously out of void.

Here's the thing that I don't understand: In improvisation, the generation of material is spontaneous, but it's never random. This in itself constitutes a paradox: If you can choose to play anything, with equal probability, what could make you choose *any one thing*—on the spur of the moment, blindly, trusting, without thinking about it—except chance? In other words, how can the spontaneous be anything *but* random; how can music made in a jolt of instinct, on a bolt out of the now, be endowed with a form that makes sense *in time*, as though it had been written and rewritten and practiced and memorized beforehand? And how, in making that first, most instinctive, most desperate decision, do we *choose*—if it really can be called "choosing," if we really choose at all?

───

Music itself begins with improvisation. Wayne Shorter, the American jazz saxophonist and composer, famously quipped that, fundamentally, "composition is just improvisation slowed down." The Hungarian musicologist Ernst Ferand wrote that "[there is] scarcely a musical technique or form of composition that did not originate in improvisatory performance or was not essentially influenced by it." This makes intuitive sense: In order to create a new piece of music, at one point you just have to start choosing notes. On the anthropological scale, long before cultural traditions of music-making existed (much less any systems for notating pitch or rhythm), it had to have been some combination of inspiration and chance that dictated what came out when humanity opened its mouth to utter those first notes of song.

As far as Western music is concerned, that began to change around the eighth century C.E., when Roman Catholic clergy invented a notation system for the modal, single-voiced Gregorian chants sung in church. From that first system, invented for the purpose of preservation and dissemination of those early airs, grew the encompassing meta-genre of classical music as we know it today, whose primary, unifying, and distinguishing trait is its literacy—"perhaps the West's signal musical distinction," as the historian and musicologist Richard Taruskin has put it. The increased accessibility of a style of music once reserved for the church and, later, the court led simultaneously to its democratization and its rarefaction, as historian Robin Moore notes in her 1992 article "The Decline of Improvisation in Western Art Music." Although improvisation remained an almost universal musical currency throughout the Baroque period and until the early Romantic period, the dissemination of written scores meant that the notes of classical music now belonged to anyone, professional or not, who could tuck a fiddle under his chin. Few amateur middle-class musicians, however, were well versed enough in the style to add the embellishments or expressive moves that make music, well, *music*. As a result, starting in the late eighteenth century, composers became more detailed and specific in their scores about what they wanted from the performer, "with all necessary ornamentation written out in an appropriate manner for those who might otherwise be unable to interpret the score improvisationally." The canonization of those written works and the establishment of conservatories for the education of professional musicians, Moore writes, caused "aspiring art musicians [to become] increasingly self-conscious in the performance of canonized works, and [they] tended to rely more heavily on the interpretative advice of influential music professionals, rather than untutored instinct"—a phenomenon that only accelerated with the advent of sound recording and, later, dubbing and editing. By this argument, it was a kind of cultural performance anxiety at large that led musicians to turn away from improvisation and toward re-creation— of the styles of famous teachers, performers, and, later, recordings—as the holy grail of classical performance. Today, the relatively fringe status of even modern, freshly composed classical music, its own genre within the genre, suggests the canon's resistance to anything truly *new*. While the last several years have seen the beginnings of a shift toward a wider embrace of contemporary music, with more and more ensembles—chamber groups especially— incorporating it into their programming alongside old warhorses by Beethoven, Schubert, Brahms, et cetera, it remains to be seen which, if any, of these works will gain a permanent canonical standing.

Yet as much as classical music (or what we think of as classical music) seems to resist the transitory, elements of improvisation remain, inextricable from the act of performance itself. The late ethnomusicologist Bruno Nettl defined improvisation as "the creation of a musical work, or the final form of a musical work, as it is being performed," noting that this "may involve the work's immediate composition by its performers, or the elaboration or adjustment of an existing framework, or anything in between. To some extent every performance involves elements of improvisation, although its degree varies according to period and place, and to some extent every improvisation rests on a series of conventions or implicit rules." Thus, a performer's spontaneous tweak to even the most minute elements of a score—a sudden heart-swell that manifests as an impromptu crescendo, an ending note held a moment longer than its allotted breath—has to it something of the improvisatory. In these terms, the latest performance of any precomposed piece becomes, in some sense, its "final form"—that is, until the next time the piece is played, because no performance can perfectly re-create the last.

It is those alterations, in fact, that constitute the high paradox of the standard of "good" classical music, and perhaps a bit of its hypocrisy. Even within the closed system of the canon, one quality strongly desired both in performer and performance is a sense of freedom—a sustained feeling of unencumbered expression, a communicable sense that your instrument is at your command as you traverse the depths and lightness of its sound. I once heard a teacher tell students in a master class that we ought to be able to get up in the middle of the night and play our Paganini études half asleep, expressively and without mistake, that's how prepared we had to be, how reliant on our muscle memory. Another instructor, kind but anxious, spent a lesson thwacking me gently on the left elbow as I played my piece from memory, murmuring, "Stop thinking, you're too tense, let it go." The model classical performer is ultraprepared and yet infinitely spontaneous, the ideal performance improvisatory but never improvised. Yet even improvisation itself, as Moore notes, "is not free," at least not completely: "It is only an effective means of expression when incorporating a vocabulary, whether cognitively or intuitively understood, common to a group of individuals." Perhaps improvisation and intensive practice, then, can be interpreted as opposite expressions of the same desire. Both seek freedom within the parameters of style and the relative constraints of form: one through preparation to the point of near oblivion, the other through a momentary oblivion that transcends any need for preparation.

It's a tension and contradiction that I could never quite reconcile in my own playing, whether

I was struggling to play all the notes just the way
I'd practiced them or attempting, and failing, to
improvise: the idea that you have to do a lot of work
in order to be considered a worthy musician, but
that if in performance it sounds as if you're having
to work for it, the music gets somehow lost. And yet
at the same time improvisation comes encumbered
with its own difficulties and anxieties; it is still gov-
erned by a sense of right and wrong in accordance
with whatever the genre dictates and, on a broader
level, what sounds reasonably decent to a human ear
trained (even through casual listening) in Western
tonality. Violin has always been like that for me:
a murky intersection of freedom and discipline,
memory and desire; the struggle to reproduce what
on the one hand I had labored mechanically to perfect in practice, what on the other hand needed to
feel free, unencumbered, alive in order to transcend
that effort and eliminate its traces from the music.
I dreaded never making something tangible; I was
afraid of the way the music passed away, that I held
it for one moment only to realize it was gone. And
that was even with music that already existed, that
I had memorized, that I could at least try to create again and again. Improvisation seemed to me a
different, more frightening thing entirely, because
the very substance of the music—here inseparable
from the act of performance itself, unlike a score—
belongs only to the moment of its creation and
therefore must die in that moment also. When I

first stumbled across the video of Montero's performance in Ruhr, it was the perfection of her music that most haunted me. I was stunned, entranced by the thought that something so complexly beautiful could have been made at a moment's thought—and, moreover, that she could be content with making something she could not pin down, that she could not create again.

That's why I ended up at the Radcliffe Institute for Advanced Study, where I'd met Aniruddh Patel a little more than a year earlier, on a sleety afternoon in Cambridge, Massachusetts, in January 2020. Montero, an elegant woman in her late forties, was there to give a talk entitled "What Choice Do I Have?" about her life as an improvisational artist. The talk was to be moderated by her husband, the Irish baritone and music producer Sam McElroy, whom she met in a coffee shop in 2010, the morning after giving a concert at the Hollywood Bowl, which he had attended. McElroy has championed his wife's gift, helping her explore the neurological roots and philosophical implications of something she doesn't know how to talk about, she says, because she doesn't understand how she does it in the first place. I attended the talk because I wanted to find out what it's like to do quite literally the opposite of everything I had ever done as a classical musician (or been taught to do), and yet to make music that sounded as though it belonged at the pinnacle of that tradition.

Montero has given interview after interview over her career about her gift, but this talk was different. With McElroy's encouragement, she had finally found some way, if not to quantify that gift itself, then to examine quantitatively what goes on in her brain when she's exercising it. She had recently been the subject of a study published in the journal *NeuroImage*, a joint effort by a team of neuroscientists, otolaryngologists, and music and sound perception researchers at Johns Hopkins and UC San Francisco. One of the lead authors, Charles Limb, has found in previous studies that improvisation strongly correlates with deactivations in the dorsal lateral prefrontal cortex, an area of the brain associated with self-awareness and, importantly, self-censorship and inhibition. Till now, Limb's research has focused primarily on neural processes in the brains of jazz musicians, for whom "improvisation forms part of their core musical behavior." He was interested in Montero precisely because she improvises in a form that, at least in some ways, wants to reject improvisation itself.

The results of the study—which consisted of having Montero play a "custom-built non-ferromagnetic piano keyboard" while lying inside an fMRI scanner—are reflected in the theme and title of her presentation at Radcliffe: *What choice do I have?* It's an idea that she has reiterated in other interviews, whenever she talks about her process: that she doesn't know what she's doing when she improvises, that it just happens, as though she is "turning on a faucet" somewhere deep inside her brain. To test why this might happen, Limb and the other researchers analyzed Montero's brain activity under three conditions, between which they asked her to switch at random. The first condition was while she played scales, the most fundamental building blocks of all music, sequences where every note is predetermined and the intervals between them follow a prescribed pattern of ascent and descent. The second was her performance of a piece she had memorized beforehand, Bach's Minuet in G—which, surprisingly enough, produced a pattern of brain activity that was largely similar to that generated by the scales, though the two tasks differed substantially in complexity. For the third and final condition, the researchers had Montero improvise in the style of the memorized Bach minuet, in order to "investigate neural correlates associated with improvisation" and how they might differ from the processes involved in the performance of memorized music. And that was where everything changed.

The difference between memorized performance and improvisation, it turns out, lies in an aspect of the brain called the default-mode network (DMN), a sprawling system of functional connectivity between regions of the brain that, loosely put, modulates the many facets of the self. These include, to name a few, the medial prefrontal cortex, which controls decision-making, self-perception, and autobiographical memory; the hippocampus, which forms new memories; the angular gyrus, a center of perception and spatial cognition, a sense of oneself in the physical world; and the dorsal medial prefrontal cortex, responsible for thoughts about others and their relation to the self. During the scale and memory trials, these areas of Montero's brain lit up with interconnectivity, as though her senses of time and space and memory were all talking to one another, working together to re-create these tasks that, together, they had been preprogrammed to execute. But each time the researchers asked Montero to switch to improvisation, the light of that interconnectivity was suddenly, substantially dimmed. (In more technical terms, the interactions between those various regions were significantly and quantifiably reduced.) If the regions of the DMN, working together, represent a unified sense of self, upon which Montero draws when she is playing music she has learned in the past, the act of improvisation somehow disbands that cohesion, requires her to draw on something else.

The DMN—not its individual regions, but as a multimodal network of interaction—tends to quiet down when the brain is involved in a task that requires deep attention to something external. An improvised musical performance provides a perfect example. The Montero study corroborates previous analyses of improvising brains, mainly those of jazz performers, which found that the "decreased self-awareness and feelings of control" that constitute a flow state are "associated with decreased activity within regions of the default-mode network." These studies have also been of extraordinary minds, but I think the phenomenon they describe has visited most of us at some point in our lives: the feeling of easy self-suspension that in the best moments can accompany deep focus, the way that when you have to throw yourself into a task it becomes almost a way to abandon the self, almost a relief to leave the self behind. The improvisation task in Montero's trial, the researchers found, resulted in decreased connectivity between the regions of the DMN overall—a momentary fracturing of the self, a temporary dissolving of its margins consistent with Montero's assertion that she "gets out of the way" when she improvises, that she loses herself in the present, that she turns on the tap and lets the music flow.

Yet the study's most interesting discovery, for me, is that something else seems to come to the fore when the conscious self deactivates. The DMN is also the seat of conscious memory, responsible for remembering the past and anticipating the future. In the intense unfurling present of improvised performance, it makes sense that thoughts of those other spheres of time might, for the moment, be abandoned. And yet the study suggests that a deeper kind of memory and anticipation may be at work. "[E]ven though GM reports that she is not conscious of what she is doing when improvising," the researchers posit, "musical motivic analysis of her improvisation trials suggests that GM often returns to musical material she had played earlier in the improvisation. Her improvisations are structured and cohesive, suggesting that her musical stream of consciousness is remarkably organized." Thus Montero's improvisations retain the shadow of things she has learned or heard or played in the past, the patterns of cadence and form imprinted on a mind constantly consumed by music. These include patterns not only of remembered auditory sequences, such as scales and arpeggios and chord progressions, but of motion internalized by her hands themselves, the motor network of her fingers "using learned patterns to create new patterns" in what the study authors call "a form of embodied creativity." Limb, who uses the term *embodied cognition*, explained to me that this is likely not the work of "a single part of the brain at all, but instead different degrees of functional interdependence between conscious thought, unconscious thought, and action/behavior that all rely on each other."

Montero's, then, is a transcendent kind of muscle memory—not one to which her musicality is bound, but, rather, which she bends to her whim and will, memory that opens up an infinity of possibilities in the present. Reading the study results reminded me of Saint Augustine's idea of *memoria*, put forth in Book X of his *Confessions:* that some things must have been there in his memory "even before I learnt them," but "remote and pushed into the background, as if in most secret caverns"; and that it is "by thinking we, as it were, gather together ideas which the memory contains in a dispersed and disordered way, and by concentrating our attention we arrange them in order as if ready to hand, stored in the very memory where previously they lay hidden, scattered, and neglected." Improvisation, then, can be seen as an uncanny manifestation of deep memory itself: the creation of order out of disorder, a deep up-pouring from some dormant part of the soul; a confirmation that "the mind knows things it does not know it knows."

Montero possesses, indeed, a keen and seemingly instantaneous musical memory: She can memorize a theme her audience sings for her after hearing it once, and immediately improvise a full-length, fully formed fantasia or fugue or concerto movement upon it. But it's more than a bolt of memorization; she seems to have an encoded, almost predestined understanding of not only the theme as it is, but of all the things it could become—a sixth sense that for most musicians could come only with extensive knowledge of a score, with a long education in music theory, with laborious and repetitive practice until the music is drilled so deep into you that you cannot forget any part of it. In other words, a sense that for most people would be anti-thetical to improvisation in the first place.

That idea of an instantaneous, prescient memory—of remembering the future, as it were—has a strange, surprising corollary in the natural world, in the universe's order of things. It's called the *path integral*, and it occurs in the realm of quantum mechanics: the sphere of the uncertain and statistical, with its tensions and overlappings between the finite and infinite, form and void. Defined by theoretical physicist Richard Feynman during the 1940s, the path integral calculates the probability that a given particle, occupying one position at a particular time, will end up at another position at a later time. The question seems simple enough, but it is complicated by the fact that quantum particles act as waves, and so their position, and the paths they take between positions, can only be described in terms of probability and not of fixity. Feynman's great insight? That a wave-particle intuits all the possible paths it could take through space and time, given the basic constraints on its movement—the time and position from which it starts, and that at which it ends—and then chooses one that is based on the sum of all those paths. And by *all possible paths* I really do mean all of them, an infinite number of journeys across the universe: The particle can take the longest path possible, and the shortest, and it can take paths of different speeds and go at different speeds within a single path. These infinite paths add up, through the superposition of their amplitudes (some of which constructively add, others of which cancel one another in whole or in part), to yield the path of least action—kinetic minus potential energy, the energy of the particle's motion minus the energy it possesses due to its position—which is the *actual* path that the particle traverses. Thus it is as though the particle, in the singular instant when it commences its motion, intuits every path it *could* take and then sets off along the one it is *destined* to take.*

Feynman himself admitted that he didn't understand why the path integral works, and I don't think it's lost on physicists that any description of the path integral necessarily ascribes not only a kind of consciousness but a prescience to the particles themselves. It implies that they know, instinctively, which path they must take in order to connect past with future, transgress the boundary of the present and link time into one chain of continuity. Similarly, when Montero improvises, it seems almost as though she is remembering the future, entraining

----

* Feynman explains the path of least action in the superb *Feynman Lectures on Physics*, a series of talks he gave at Cal Tech from 1961 to 1963 and which were later adapted into a celebrated physics textbook, a sort of layman's bible for explanations of physical phenomena. "We can calculate the kinetic energy minus the potential energy and integrate for such a path . . . or for any other path we want. The miracle is that the true path is the one for which that integral is least."

to something that doesn't yet exist. She intuits all the possibilities contained within a single theme, between its notes, inside its silences . . . and then picks one path to follow, plucks one shimmering thread from the tangle of possibilities and follows where it leads. The principle of least action manifests itself in her improvisations, then, not in that she plays what's easiest; rather, that she plays what occurs to her to play, what comes as she lets herself drift along with time. She doesn't think or resist; she just *does*, leaning into the predestiny of form.

When Montero was seventeen, she quit the piano. She was discouraged by the teacher who had told her to stop improvising, and by the relentlessness of the competitions and concerts that until then had regimented her life, giving it a punishing kind of order: "I thought, this doesn't really mean anything, this isn't really my own choice, this isn't really me."* It was a time of intense alienation from herself, where "I actually pretty much hated music at that point, I hated being a prisoner of my own nature, and I hated not having any other options." And so she closed the lid of the piano. During that period of silence, she tried to figure out what she wanted to do with her life, what she would dedicate

---

* This and all subsequent quotes of Montero's are from her lecture at Radcliffe, a recording of which can be found at: https://www.radcliffe.harvard.edu/event/what-choice-do-i-have-gabriela-montero-discusses-classical-improvisation-composition-and-creative-dissent.

it to if not music. She wanted to do something that would "contribute to society"; she thought she might try going into social work. Yet a few years later, almost in spite of herself, she sent in an old recording as an audition tape for the Royal Academy of Music in London. She was accepted, which, she says, "somehow put me on the path again of music." While at the Academy, she had the option to study "basic theoretical subjects" in music, like harmony and solfege, but none of them appealed to her. "It was not something that I processed intellectually in the same way that others would," she told the audience at Radcliffe. "For me it was all about the emotional relationship, and reactionary relationship, to the instrument."

"So it was almost as though music was a language that didn't require a second language to describe it," McElroy said. "It just *was*."

Montero smiled. "Yeah, exactly. It always was. It always was."

What choice, then, do I have? That question—with its dual implications of helplessness and power—has inflected nearly every part of Montero's life in music. She began concertizing again, this time incorporating improvisation into her programs, after a chance encounter with the legendary classical pianist Martha Argerich in the early 2000s. After hearing Montero improvise in a Montreal hotel, Argerich looked at her and said, "This is so special, Gabi, why aren't you sharing this with the world?" Montero didn't know how to reply. "Just do it," Argerich told her. That encounter, and Montero's subsequent launch into a full-blown international career, provided a platform for what Montero says is the most important part of her work as an artist: her activism against the authoritarian regime in Venezuela, which began when she refused to perform for a government-sponsored concert in 2004. She was a single mother at that time, with "a thousand dollars in the bank"; she was told that if she played the concert she would "never have to worry about money again." Montero responded that she didn't have a price. She began using her concerts and recordings as platforms to educate international audiences about what was happening in Venezuela—the soaring murder rates, the kidnappings and ransoms, the deaths from starvation under the increasingly brutal and despotic regimes of Hugo Chávez and Nicolás Maduro—and to warn of the insurgence of what she calls a "mafia state." Now, she and McElroy, who live in Barcelona, help as many refugees as they can, funding and organizing their escapes from Venezuela and giving them a home until they are back on their feet. "It's a matter of time before truths are revealed," Montero said, "and before we understand a history." In this work, especially, she feels she has no choice: to do what she can for whom she can, up against the void of a system that has utterly collapsed. As with her improvisations, it's a question of order mediated by chance, or perhaps the other way around: The knowledge that anything could happen pulls against the deep convicted sense that it has to be this way only; from within the infinite dark parameters the choosing of this one true thing.

In physics, our ability to remember the past but not the future has a name: the "arrow of time," famously described by Stephen Hawking in *A Brief History of Time: From the Big Bang to Black Holes.* This "psychological arrow,"* as Hawking deemed it—the asymmetry of our knowledge of ourselves in time, the weighted imbalance of memory—has two counterparts, two additional arrows that constitute our sense of time's forward direction but are external to human consciousness. One arrow is entropy itself, the spontaneous, irreversible process by which the disorder of closed systems increases according to the second law of thermodynamics. This is responsible for the decay that mars and makes up ordinary life, from the aging of cells to the fracturing of families; one of the most well-worn examples used in physics is an eggshell, which can break but not re-form. The other arrow constitutes the direction of the universe's expansion outward from the Big Bang, entropy unspooling on the scale of the

---

* Hawking discusses the idea at length in Chapter 9 of *A Brief History of Time*, "The Arrow of Time" (p. 182–195).

cosmos. Hawking argued that the very formation of human memory inevitably increases the entropy of the universe: that the energy required to align the neurons in charge of creating and storing memories, which is used up and dissipated as heat, will always exceed the minute gain in order represented by the creation of an individual memory itself. Thus the direction in which we remember our lives *is* the direction in which entropy increases; every point in our psychological past corresponds, always, to a time when the universe, in its entirety, was more ordered than it is now.

I used to think that improvisation embodied its own arrow of time in some ways. An act of improvisation is not only irreversible but unrepeatable; once it's been played, the music cannot exist in the same way again. This seems particularly true when it is juxtaposed against the canon of precomposed classical music, whose very existence seems constructed to defy entropy, to enclose time and seal it off so that it cannot trickle linearly away, to ensure that we remember. As a written score opens up possibilities of structure and complexity—the capacity for a piece of music to contain a higher level of disorder—so, too, has classical music, as a canon and a practice, been designed to ward off the entropic force of time as more and more music is written, as the world's disorder increases, as time itself moves onward. In the neurological realm, the brain's default-mode network seems designed to fight entropy within itself and thus to keep the self in order, to organize the various aspects of the mind that it governs and keep them confined to their designated functions. "Entropy is a dimensionless quantity that is used for measuring uncertainty about the state of a system[,] but it can also imply physical qualities, where high entropy is synonymous with high disorder,"* write the neurologist Robin Carhart-Harris and his team in a 2014 paper entitled "The Entropic Brain: A Theory of Conscious States Informed by Neuroimaging Research with Psychedelic Drugs," published in *Frontiers in Neuroscience*. Carhart-Harris, a neurologist at Imperial College London, studies the effects of psychedelic substances on human consciousness; in the 2014 study, he and his team found that the drug psilocybin caused "a collapse of the normally highly organized activity with the default-mode network (DMN)"—a collapse that, in turn, produced a state of "unconstrained cognition and less ordered (high-entropy) neurodynamics." That quantifiable decentralization of self is the same phenomenon that Limb measured, five years later, in Gabriela Montero's improvising brain. (Another study by researchers at Imperial College, the Guildhall School of Music of Drama, and the

---

* Carhart-Harris, Robin Lester, et al. "The Entropic Brain: A Theory of Conscious States Informed by Neuroimaging Research with Psychedelic Drugs." Frontiers in Human Neuroscience 8 (2014): 17. doi:10.3389/fnhum.2014.00020.

Tokyo Institute of Technology in 2018, though not focused on the DMN specifically, found increases in brain entropy overall when classical performers improvised rather than played from a score.*) The drug of improvisation, like drugs of altered consciousness, seems to open up associative pathways along which the self is given permission to disintegrate, to give in to the pull of disorder and its accompanying freedoms.

And yet improvisation, as evinced by the structure and organization of Montero's performances, is far from a succumbing to randomness. In fact, when seen through another lens, improvisation looks not like order unraveling but order restored, more a path integral than an arrow of time. The irreversibility is there, yes, the singular momentariness; but there's also the sense that the improviser is creating a form that holds up in time and makes sense in it, with a beginning and an end that lead, and then lead back to, each other. That's what I hear when Montero plays, anyway: the simultaneity of time embodied by the path integral, whereby a particle traverses freely the terrain of past, present, future, and renders those boundaries meaningless. Thus improvisation, or at least Montero's

---

* David Dolan et al.,"The Improvisational State of Mind: A Multidisciplinary Study of an Improvisatory Approach to Classical Music Repertoire Performance," *Frontiers in Psychology*, 9 (2018):1341, doi:10.3389/fpsyg.2018.01341.

improvisations, may serve as a metaphor for time in the quantum universe, where reality and possibility exist simultaneously and where past, present, and future are one—even though on the level of concrete, lived experience time seems to slip away, to vanish, without the possibility of return.

And yet in life there is, from time to time, a sense of looping back, for all of us; the sense that time itself may not be as linear, entropic, random as it seems. The sequence of random luck and chance encounters that led Montero back to music, even after she had decided she was done—the decision, on a whim, to apply to the Royal Academy; her chance meeting with Martha Argerich; the moment she and McElroy locked eyes in a Los Angeles Starbucks—become, under a different frame of reference, the story of how things were always meant to be. Time exists as narrative; memory, too, is not only entropic but improvisatory. We necessarily lose fragments of it, our memories alter, are drained of life, or take on new significances to which we either reduce or inflate them. Time renders most individual moments meaningless, or at least less important than they originally seemed, but it is only through the passage of time that life acquires its meaning. And that meaning itself is constantly in flux; we are always making it up and then revising as we go along, ordering and reordering our understanding of the past in real time. If nothing else, improvisation manifests the human rage to create, as time passes, a narrative that can expand to include all of experience as it is lived and render it logical, ordered, as it was meant to be.

In the study of Montero's brain, the researchers noted that, though the flow states brought on by deactivation of the DMN generally represent a momentary suspension of ego, "artists like GM also call on their emotions and personal identity when performing"—even if these emotions are not "the primary subject of conscious thought." Even when she was a child, Montero recalled at Radcliffe, "for me the piano was always a very emotional tool. The piano was always my friend, that I would tell stories to. I would always arrive at the piano and the first thing I would do would be to improvise, it's just the most natural and intimate thing that I can do, and the most powerful, emotional language that I can use to describe how I feel, what I've been through, what I see around me. And that was always there from the beginning." She smiled. "For me, improvisation was always just a way to narrate life."

At this point in the presentation, McElroy surprised Montero: He had secretly brought along one of many tape recordings her mother had made of her improvising as a little girl. It was of an elementary school–aged Montero playing a little composition called "The Wild Horsemen," and McElroy asked her "far older self to improvise on your younger self" for the audience. Grinning, he pressed PLAY to activate the recording, "which," he said to Montero, "you will not have heard since you composed it." It was a dark piece, moody and martial, but above the somberness of the chords you could hear the voice of a child singing, picking out the tune while telling the story to herself.

As Montero listened, she began to smile. "Well, you see how truthful my husband is in saying that he did not tell me [he was going to ask me to do] this," she said as the recording played, "because what he doesn't realize is that's actually Schumann!" McElroy had accidentally chosen what, Montero said, laughing, was "probably the only [childhood recording] that *wasn't* my improvisation." It was a tune from Robert Schumann's *Album for the Young*, a book of miniature pieces that he wrote for his three young daughters in 1848, and it was indeed called "The Wild Horseman." "My God," Montero said, chuckling, "I literally have not played this since I was what, six or seven?" She seated herself at the keyboard and lightly fingered the theme, mystically, thoughtfully, looking upward. There was something tender about it, somehow; watching her there, it was easy to imagine her, suddenly, as a little girl. She began to play, and a slow Baroque-style fugue unrolled itself from her fingertips, transfiguring the theme into a relic of an even older time. She was improvising upon Schumann, yes, but also upon her childhood self, the fragments of things lost and remembered. To create is indeed to remember; to remember is to involve oneself in a universe of feeling, to fold time in on itself until it can contain itself no longer. That first suddenness, and the ensuing flow; river of fire, mouth of ecstasy, the singular moment of fission and rapture. Was it some higher plan, or else the great dice-throw of the cosmos: the creation of form like the breaking of silence, a big bang emanating out into space over the face of the deep, just as in the beginning was the song.

Symmetry Breaking

*[A]rt, like life, is inclined to mitigate,
to loosen, to modify, even to break strict
symmetry. But seldom is asymmetry
merely the absence of symmetry. Even in
asymmetric designs one feels symmetry as
the norm from which one deviates under the
influence of forces of non-formal character.*

—Hermann Weyl, *Symmetry*

It is a winter's night, I am seventeen. I have gone
to wake her up, as I have the last several nights this
week. It's 1:00 A.M., and the house is still; she is
scrunched at the edge of the bed, in the rumpled
margin that little Aidan has left her, wedged into
the angle formed by his arm and his sleep-skewed
hip. She falls asleep here, sometimes, after putting
him to bed, patting his back until he falls asleep.
He sleeps diagonally, limbs splayed out. She doesn't
move him for fear of waking him. He's only five; he
doesn't know how lightly and restlessly she sleeps,
how few her moments of respite are.

It is one of those rare moments now, I think,
peering down at her in the blue winter dark.

Though she has hardly any room, teetering on the precipice of the bed's edge, she is breathing with the deep, relieved sound of someone whose only privacy is in sleep. Her brow is smoothed over by the night. The window by the bed is webbed with spidery cracks, shimmery with refracted streetlamp light. In the half-glow that enters the room, I study the landscape of her face: the mild and weary valleys beneath her eyes, the shadows that pool there from a buried sorrow.

I hesitate before reaching down to wake her—my hand, puppet of my own need, flexes and stalls in the dark. She was so tired today. The five-year-old doesn't know what I know, that she will rouse herself at five thirty, a few hours from now and an hour before everyone else. The early morning will be brittle with cold. She will turn on the stove and cook breakfast with stiff fingers as the blue flames soften the kitchen air, enduring the gradual, bitter thaw so that when her children wake up the house will be warm.

The little pendulum on the clock in Aidan's room swings back and forth. Will you wake her, or will you let her sleep? Will you be a selfish daughter or a good one? It flicks the seconds away: impatient, indifferent.

I study her again. Her breathing is so soft. Even in sleep she is discreet, self-effacing. Let her at least have this to herself.

And still, I lean down and whisper, "Uhmma, will you practice with me?"

——

My mother also grew up playing the violin, although for her it wasn't exactly a matter of choice. The public school music program in Arvada—the suburb of Denver to which her family immigrated after leaving Seoul in 1966—offered free orchestra classes and use of its janky collection of instruments, so it just made sense for her to join. Besides, her parents wanted her to play; they both loved classical music, even though they couldn't afford to give her lessons or a violin of her own. She was nine years old when she started, which, unless you are a prodigy, is too late if you want to become a professional violinist. The daughter of a close family friend, a Korean girl my mother's age, had started violin when she was two and eventually went on to study at Juilliard; she was playing the Mozart concertos when my mother was just learning "Hot Cross Buns." By eighth grade, my mother was able to start private lessons; in high school, she finally got her own violin, for three hundred dollars (the average price of even a factory-made student instrument is usually a couple of thousand). It wasn't an option for her *not* to quit, either, after a certain point in time: She was working so much in high school, after her father passed away, that by her senior year there was simply not enough time for her to continue playing the violin.

This, then, is the immigrant credo: to be able to give your children what you did not have yourself. All four of us have played since we were about five, Eloise and Eliot and Aidan and me: Eloise and I the violin, Eliot the cello, and Aidan, the youngest, both violin and viola. We grew up practicing every day except for Christmas, and we didn't think about it much; it was just what one did. Regimented daily practice—consisting of scales and arpeggios, études, new pieces, and "review" pieces, always in that order—was encouraged by Denver Talent Education (DTE), the Saturday program for "Suzuki kids" and their "Suzuki parents"* that Mom started taking us to when I was about seven and my sister five. It was held in a cavernous Lutheran church in South Denver, which on those mornings bustled with over a hundred students toting miniature violins and cellos and violas. Many of them were Asian, or half Asian like us; and, like us, if they were halfies, it was almost always their Asian parent who accompanied them. It was a beautiful thing, actually, now that I look back on it, all these little

---

* Developed by pedagogue Shinichi Suzuki in the middle of the twentieth century, the Suzuki Method is an international curriculum of instrument playing that applies "the basic principles of language acquisition to the learning of music," and which is based on the belief that, with the "loving encouragement" of a parent, "every child can learn" to play an instrument. See "About the Suzuki Method," suzukiassociation.org.

kids playing "Twinkle, Twinkle, Little Star" and its thousand variations in unison. For me, the fun was in being there with my mom. I felt proud as I played, knowing she was watching me, reassured by her presence. It was our special time together, those Saturday mornings. One time, she left briefly during one of my group classes to get something from the car or to check on Eloise (who was more independent and never needed Mom to sit in on her classes). I wept as we played one of the themes from *Judas Maccabaeus*, a chorus of tiny violins squeaking out the melody by Handel. The teacher, a smiley woman in her thirties, hurried over to my spot in the circle. "Are we feeling a little weak this morning?" she whispered kindly. I let out another gasping sob and continued to play.

And so it was never about the regimen only. I should note here, lest a sense (and illusion) of complete drudgery take over, that we loved music. For my siblings and me, in fact, the whole world *was* music, and music was color: the sound of a jackhammer at work in the C- major light of early morning, alternating in deep tones between the pitches A and B on the pavement; the blackish purple E-flat of a plane's engine revving; the blue birdsong outside the window of the room my sister and I shared.* When Eloise was three or four and didn't know the lyrics to songs, she would sing the names of each pitch instead, something both of us were born knowing how to recognize. Mom loved this, and marveled at it. I used to tell her, during our Suzuki practice, what color represented each key signature in the Bach Double or Corelli's "La Folia," and we would use this to help me memorize the order of the various sections and modulations. She had her own metaphors and images for the music, too: the snowstorm section, the ascending line like the flight of birds, the section like a prayer. When I play or listen to these pieces now, twenty years later, hers are the metaphors that come to mind, the colors that I hear. I say all this now because, in that early unself-conscious beginning, I loved music because music was how I perceived the world, in a synesthetic collision of one

---

* Synesthesia, which has been estimated to affect anywhere from one in two hundred to one in twenty thousand people, occurs when "the stimulation of one [sensory] modality simultaneously produces sensation in a different modality." See Palmeri et al., "What is synesthesia?" scientificamerican.com. Common sensory interactions and interfaces include associating numbers and letters with specific colors (grapheme-color synesthesia) and sounds with colors (chromesthesia); visualizing numerical sequences as shaped arrangements in space (spatial-sequence synesthesia); and perceiving words as having distinct tastes (lexical-gustatory synesthesia).

sense with another, one love with another. And at the center of that world was Mom.

Even at that age I apprehended something of how much she wanted to give me. I just didn't know the extent or the cost. I remember her getting me ready for a DTE concert once, when I was a little older; it was Christmastime, and all of the students were supposed to dress up in black and white and red. Uhmma had bought me a red dress, bright as D major, with a bow on the front. She smiled at me, her eyes filled with pride, as she fastened the buttons and smoothed the full skirt. And I remember that, for some reason I can't explain, I made a mean face and stamped my foot in its shiny black Mary Jane shoe—clear-eyed and without anger, in that experimental way kids have of being cruel; just to see, out of curiosity, how much I could hurt her.

She gives, I take: that has always been the imbalanced equation of our relationship, its asymmetry and equilibrium. The year in which this story begins and ends, the year I was seventeen, I was caught up in a rage of becoming: a nightly routine of practicing violin until 2:00 or 3:00 A.M., only allowing myself to stop once my arms felt useless and my eyes were closing beyond resistance. I practiced in what we called "the library," a little room that housed two symmetrical bookshelves on either side of a defunct fireplace. To the right of the shelves was the mirror, and I would stand in front of it and watch myself as I practiced my violin, the open window behind me: my world of night, a landscape of reflected things. If I stood at a certain angle, I could see the black-and-white picture of my mother's father—"Harabuji," we called him, which is Korean for grandfather—looking back at me from one of the shelves. On another, the photograph of him and my grandmother with my aunt, who was nine, and my mother, who was only three, on the day they arrived in America from Seoul.

Every night that year, before she put Aidan to bed, Mom would offer me her help, tell me to wake her up if she fell asleep and I needed her. I shouldn't have awakened her, those bitter almost-mornings when the house was still, those rare times when she didn't need to be anywhere but where she was, when no one was clamoring for her attention, battering her with yet another litany of needs. And yet, come midnight or 1:00 A.M., I inevitably found myself tiptoeing upstairs and into Aidan's room—why I took such pains to be quiet in the moments before I woke her, I don't know—and reaching down to touch her shoulder. She slept so lightly that it never took much to wake her. My justifications were whispered, rushed, and many: "This passage isn't going right, I can't get these double-stops in tune, I can't hear if the phrasing makes sense from an audience perspective, could you come listen and tell me if it sounds all right?" I would wake her up under the guise of needing her help because I felt too guilty to say what I really meant: that I hated being alone in the dark, that I needed her to be adrift with me. I think I justified it to myself in part because I knew it made her happy that I played and played well; I wanted to show her how hard I was working and that I didn't take my lessons for granted, and, more than anything, to validate her sacrifice, feeling beholden even though I knew she had never asked that repayment of me.

I guess I've never been able to help myself. I love her, and in loving her I define her as *my* mother, the woman who has devoted her life to my siblings and me. As I get older, it seems to me that trying to learn how to love somebody the right way—to give enough of yourself, but never too much—is to discover the frightening asymmetry at the heart of love. Like a kaleidoscope that, twisted relentlessly in the hands of a child, establishes a crystalline moment of symmetry only to be broken again, changed to something new, the work of love lays bare the infirmity of the divide between past and future, self and other, you and I. Why do those symmetries, which ought to be so set in stone, break and re-form and break again, and in doing so make selflessness and self-preoccupation impossible to tell apart from one another?

Other people liked to look at Mom's sacrifices and take her selflessness literally—literally, as in they concluded that she must not have a self. "Isn't your mom sort of a Tiger Mom?" a high school friend once asked me, a Caucasian friend who also played violin. This was 2012, and America was still up in arms against Amy Chua's memoir *Battle Hymn of the Tiger Mother*, which had been excerpted in *The Wall Street Journal* the previous year under the headline WHY CHINESE MOTHERS ARE SUPERIOR. My mother is Korean, but by then the book's central term, *Tiger Mother*, had already made its way into common parlance, swallowing up every mom who looked like mine: an Asian woman who raises her children to excel in academics and classical music, essentially by forcing them to practice well and study hard. Much of the backlash was against how Chua often took tiger-mothering to the extreme, threatening to burn or donate her young daughters' toys if they didn't practice or learn their pieces well enough. Our mom never did anything like that. Still, white mothers would come up to my siblings and me after recitals, and after a few moments of lighthearted complimentary chatter would inevitably exclaim, "I just don't know how your mom can be so good at getting you to practice!" and, almost in irritation, "Don't you think she should spend more time on herself?" Once, after a community-orchestra concert at which I performed Saint-Saëns's Violin Concerto No. 3 in B minor, a woman with a highlight-streaked perm, breathless and clutching a purple snakeskin handbag, cornered me as I left the dressing room. "I have kids who play, too," she said, "not as well, of course, I mean I can never get them to practice, but I also don't want to, you know, be *overbearing*. Your mom must make you practice all the time . . ." As I left the church with Mom, holding my violin and the flowers she had brought for me, the kind county policeman serving as concert security saw my mother and exclaimed, in an amiable jolt of recognition—"Oh, so you're a *half-breed*!"—and wished us good night.

In retrospect, focusing our lives so singularly on classical music was indeed the most stereotypically Asian thing we could have done, we were picture-perfect in that way: four hapa children trailed by our Korean mother to orchestra concerts and rehearsals, each of us with a black instrument case strapped to his or her back. And yet, except during those occasional moments of insinuation or insult, the music itself never felt racialized.* Everything, for me, was just about getting good at the violin. As soon as we would get in the car after a performance, I would turn to my mother and grill her about what had gone well and what I could

---

* This is not the case for many Asian musicians, of course, particularly when performing in Europe, the birthplace of Western classical music and almost all its canonical composers. The cellist Yo-Yo Ma, in a 2020 interview with David Marchese for *The New York Times Magazine*, recalled that "[w]hen I started playing concerts on a regular basis in my early 20s, in Europe the most often asked question was, 'How can an Oriental like you understand music?'"

have done better, demanding her critique and its ego-satisfying proof of her attention. What could be more affirming for a child than to be conscious of your parent's singular devotion to this thing that you love, that you have chosen to make your life?

Mom didn't have that herself, of course, not after her father died. Her own mother—our grandmother, Halmoni—loved her daughters but was hands-off as a parent, partly because she suffered from severe depression, and partly because she, too, had to work multiple jobs after her husband passed away. Sometimes, my mom told me, her mother would come home from work and go straight into her bedroom; Mom and her older sister could hear the murmur of the television through the locked door. On those nights, the two of them would clean the house and make the rice before finishing their homework.

There is a Korean phrase, *"yeolsimhi il hagehsseumnidah,"* that is proclaimed with a deep and earnest bow whenever one undertakes something new: "I will work hard; I will do my best." The only thing, my mother told me, in which she'd had a choice after her father died was in how hard she worked. She stayed up until two or three in the morning on a daily basis, perfecting her homework after coming home from cheerleading or orchestra practice or the five different clubs of which she was president, and then from the restaurant at which she waited tables. As a result, the counselor at

Arvada West High School called my grandmother in on multiple occasions to voice her genuine bewilderment and concern that something was wrong: "We've just—we've never had a student *work* so hard before. Does she eat? Does she rest?" In the car on the way home, my grandmother would roll her eyes and sigh, "Sunhee, can't you just get a B?"

Mom told me this story long ago, and I hear echoes of it in the Tiger Mother accusations that are lobbed not only at her but at Asian-American mothers in general. Chua's book sparked a small culture war in 2011, a furious back-and-forth of interviews and op-eds—not to mention the racist emails and death threats Chua received—about the "right" way to parent in America. One of the most common criticisms of Chua's parenting model was voiced by sociologist Christine Carter in *The Huffington Post*, who wrote that "Chua is prescribing life motivated by perfectionism—fear of failure, fear of disappointment," which can only lead to "a vicious form of unhappiness" for children of Asian-style parenting. Ayelet Waldman voiced a similar sentiment, albeit more humorously, in her article "In Defense of the Guilty, Ambivalent, Preoccupied Western Mom," a *Wall Street Journal* rebuttal to Chua, where she acknowledged that her own children were "always allowed" to "[q]uit the piano and the violin, especially if their defeatist attitude coincided with a recital, thus saving me from the torture of listening to other people's precious children soldier through hackneyed pieces of the juvenile repertoire, plink after ever more unbearable plonk."

Is there something to be said for letting kids quit, fail, and find their way on their own? Surely. Yet what these criticisms miss, for me, is the way that Chua's methods, codified as they are into the American stereotype of the relentlessly task-mastering Asian mother, are both germane to the immigrant experience and revealing of its burden. "We have to be twice as good to be considered half as much," a Korean friend of my mother's once told her in college. And she was right: For Asian parents in America, the "fear of failure, fear of disappointment" is doubly fraught. For the price of being labeled a "Tiger Mother," they can remain faithful to Eastern philosophies of parenting and fulfill what they deem to be their basic responsibilities to their children—or they can adopt a more laissez-faire Western approach in the name of assimilation, and in doing so cut ties with their cultural past. (And it is our American reality, too, that the children of wealthy white parents can afford to experiment with failure more than others.) Thus the urgency of raising successful children becomes even more exacerbated and more complicated for the Asian mother in America, and for her child. Fail to make the most of your opportunity, and all your family's sacrifice was for naught; bang your head against the wall and seize that chance with all your strength, and even though you'll add your own nameless face to the swelling flesh of the stereotype you'll at least have found some way to survive, if never to belong.

Nowhere is this more apparent than with the Asian parent/classical music stereotype, an image that is fraught because it is largely true. Musicians of Asian descent, almost always propelled by parental sacrifice and effort, make up anywhere between 15 and 40 percent of the undergraduate populations at the top conservatories in the United States, such as Juilliard and the Curtis Institute of Music. Yet, according to a 2016 diversity report conducted by the League of American Orchestras, only about 9 percent of professional orchestral musicians identify as Asian or Pacific Islander. Indeed, the predominating group in classical music remains Caucasian, and the scholar Mari Yoshihara, in her 2007 book *Musicians from a Different Shore*, is quick to note the implications of that asymmetry between image and reality—that "[s]uch an exaggerated perception of Asian dominance in classical music suggests that Asian musicians are racially marked." "Because classical music is associated with Western high culture and because the performance of classical music requires many years of disciplined training," she writes, "Asians' success in this field is often thought to exemplify their assimilation into Euro-american culture," their incorporation into a "model minority: those who rise in the existing social structure through hard work and attain success in Western culture without posing a direct challenge to the economic and political status quo."

What happens, then, when the desire to assimilate runs up against the desire to assert an individual voice? The problem with playing classical music when you're young—even if you don't have a choice in the matter—is often that, eventually, you can't help but love it. This is by no means true for everyone, but for those of us for whom it is—all of a sudden you can't get enough; it leaves you dizzy and breathless, drunk, almost, on your obsession; and then even though you know you are playing directly into the stereotype you have no choice but to keep going. You *can't* quit, not now that you love it, and not after so much investment on your part and the part of your parents, the anguish of so many shared and sleepless nights.

Yet as many Asian-Americans as there are who go into classical music, an equal number have no choice but to lay their instruments down and walk away. My mother is one of this latter group. She quit violin her senior year of high school, in order to focus on working and getting into college. "There wouldn't have been a chance anyway—I wasn't that great," she'd always say. "But the one thing I did have going for me was my bow hold. There was this trumpet teacher, actually, who taught me first, at school—and for some reason he knew how to teach a perfect violin bow hold." She laughed and shook her head. "It was bizarre. But it helped me get up to the Mozart concertos. Beyond that, I couldn't really do it anymore—my technique was too deficient, I had started so late, and my instrument was so limiting."

I know now, as I write this, that it's going to sound as though my mother saw in me the resurrection of her dead dream, the vehicle by which I would fulfill a broken promise of a life in music. But that's not it, that cannot be it, because hers was never a desperate devotion, nor a self-serving, self-seeking one. She did make us practice, but it wasn't so that we would reflect well on her; she always stayed in the background after our lessons and concerts, waiting discreetly in the shadows for us to finish talking to our teachers and the conductors and audience members. It's more, I think, that she wanted us to feel as if we were good at something and would have the choice to keep going if *we* wanted to, that we wouldn't be fettered by a bad instrument or a technique developed too little or too late, that if eventually we did walk away we wouldn't feel the regret of wondering, perhaps, whether we could have worked harder. She had felt the twinge of that regret herself, but even after she gave up music, she couldn't really look back; there wasn't time. She made it into Harvard, where she majored in English and worked shifts in the serving line at the freshman dining hall in a plastic hairnet. After college, out of practicality rather than desire, she went to law school and became a lawyer, federal

prosecutor, and administrative law judge (her ful-
fillment of that other Asian stereotype, she jokes
sometimes).

Dad—who looked so vulnerable when she saw
him coming through the courtyard arch that day
in April of her senior year at Harvard, sniffing his
underarm when he thought no one was looking—
well, he descended from a different world: a crys-
tal sphere of silver coffee spoons and North Shore
cocktail parties awash with murmurs and tinkling
laughter, blue-blooded New Englanders who moved
in endless easy circles from St. Paul's to Harvard to
Martha's Vineyard and then back again, buoyed by
their confidence in that mysterious and intangible
birthright. His parents, a private wealth manager
and an heiress from Essex, Massachusetts, had
been shocked, to say the least, when their son mar-
ried "an Oriental." I imagine my mother moving
through the velvet crowd on Dad's arm, the empty,
lofty faces greeting his and barely registering hers.
If she weren't standing with him—maybe waiting
for him to come back from glad-handing his parents' friends and his old classmates from St. Paul's,
standing solitarily off to the side in the black dress
she scrimped for months to buy so she wouldn't
embarrass him—sometimes people would come up
to her, the only Asian amid a sea of WASPy white,
and hand her their empty wineglasses or ask her to
take their coats. I imagine her trying to seem at
ease, concentrating too hard on the quartet music

playing in the background, longing silently to be seen yet afraid that someone would see her and call her out for what she was: an impostor. Her mistake was thinking that she might find some protection in the storied enclosure of Dad's family, whose name would protect her future children from discrimination and in whose expansive sense of noblesse oblige there must surely be room to embrace an immigrant like her. When he asked her to marry him in 1988—even though she had her reservations by then, even though when she got in a scooter crash that nearly killed her he didn't so much as turn up at the hospital—who was she, she asked me once, sobbing, to say no to someone like him?

Dad decided to leave our family in the fall of 2016, to marry a woman from Massachusetts with a pedigree more symmetrical to his. When he left, he said he had to do it, that he had never loved Mom, and he accused her of being mentally ill, flying around the country trying to get her diagnosed by psychiatrists behind her back. The illness he accused her of, in his words, was "being a perfectionist mother." He had always hated our involvement in music in particular; he thought it smacked of "middle-class" immigrant striving. (In fairness, but mostly to please him, Mom had us try soccer and lacrosse, which he had played, but none of us loved either sport; I, for one, was an embarrassment on both fields.) I still hear his voice sometimes, when I am getting into the car with my violin: the way he would sneer, "There goes the Momager" as we left the house for a quartet gig, Eloise and I laden with our instruments and foldable music stands, Mom with the massive blue canvas bag that held our music binders and rehearsal notepads and everything else we might need—clothespins to secure the music to the stand if the gig was outside on a windy day, extra hairpins and black clothes just in case. He used to smack us on the head, Eliot most of all, if we annoyed him by singing or whis- tling in the house, or said "thank you" too much. Once, when Eliot was not yet two, Dad yanked on his arm so hard that his elbow popped out of its socket. I remember the way it lay skewed, at an angle, in the sleeve of his yellow footed pajamas. I didn't realize till later, however, what violence Mom had endured: that the time she took us to a motel— "just for the night, don't worry, we'll see Daddy tomorrow"—was because she was so afraid; that when she couldn't walk a couple weeks after baby Eliot was born it was not because she'd fallen, as she told everyone, but because he had hit her so hard that the stitches from her cesarean burst. Even so, she didn't feel she had any choice but to stay with him, because Denver courts almost always divide child custody symmetrically, fifty-fifty between both parents, even if one parent has abused his or her spouse or child, and so she knew what a divorce would mean: that at his house, on his time, there would be no buffer between him and us.

How differently it turned out than she must have imagined. I know she always wanted to have kids, to make her children her life; she has told me that. She just didn't know what it would cost. I know she is willing to endure it, that she has always been willing to endure anything for our sakes. But I can also imagine how it must be hard sometimes, when the house is dark and she is the last one awake and the dishes she washed by hand that morning are piled up again in the sink, and she crawls into bed knowing that it will all be waiting for her in the morning, the mounting debt, the emails from Dad threatening to go back to court to get more time with Aidan, and the panic in little Aidan's eyes when she wakes him because he is afraid to go over to Dad's—how hard it must be to think that yes, this is my life.

When I first began writing this chapter, I thought I would focus on equality, or really the lack thereof, in my mother's experience of America, embodied as it is in her relationship with my father and his family and even, to some extent, with us, her children. And yet as I wrote I realized that equality was not exactly what I meant, that this word was not precise enough to pinpoint the difficulty of my mother's experience as an immigrant, or the pang of guilt and gratitude I felt watching her as she mopped and swept the floors, scrimped frantically to save money for my violin lessons, rushed to get dinner on the table before Dad got home while I fiddled away in front of the mirror, an instrument tucked under my chin.

Equality describes an external relationship between separate entities: between Asians and Caucasians, husbands and wives, parents and their children. In my mother's experience of assimilation, at least, there was never any point in discussing equality in relation to white people. It was more about scraping by, striking an impossible balance between making sure you didn't stand out enough to get picked on and doing well enough that you weren't automatically passed over, cast aside. The fact that the children of so many Asian immigrants play classical music at a disproportionately high level—that they excel in a genre at the dusty peak of Western high art, one in which contemporary American culture is increasingly less interested—has made it an "Asian thing," an Asian stereotype, a manifestation of that stubborn will to work that marks a certain kind of perceived inferiority. The performance of identity, especially that of a "model minority," rarely, if ever, lends itself to notions of equality: In trying to play the part society has prescribed for you, you are inherently left at the mercy of the people who are watching, auditioning you for their way of life, evaluating whether or not you belong.

Instead, it is symmetry—from the Greek *symmetria*, "agreement in dimensions, due proportion, arrangement"—that offers, to my mind, a more apt metaphor for assimilation, because symmetry describes the relationship of a single identity to itself. Every personal identity is an entity in flux, a constant negotiation of the multitude of more specific identities that it comprises and their myriad proportions to one another. Wife and mother, parent and child, Korean and American: Each of us has the capacity to become a slightly different person, depending on where we are and whom we are with, in any given moment of interaction. The balance of who we are is determined by the symmetries and asymmetries of those identities, the relationship, forged by their interplay, between how others see us and how we see ourselves. Should she support our music, or appease her husband? Should she be an Asian mother or an American one?

Assimilation—perhaps more than any other crisis of identity—threatens to throw that balance out of whack. Its grief begins when you notice that the way others perceive you has begun to diverge from the way you see yourself. For my mother, that divergence was always palpable: in sidelong looks, in people moving away from her at the post office or the grocery store; in the man who slapped her across the face while she was walking down the street in Denver her freshman year of college, screaming, "You dirty yellow thing, taking jobs away from good American people." Decades later, it wounded her identity as a mother when people asked her children if she was a Tiger Mother. How were we supposed to respond? She started all four of us in classical music at age five; she was our first teacher, and she required that we practice every day. She wanted us to play so that we would learn how to work hard and discipline ourselves when undertaking a task, to help us get into good colleges, to give us a chance. How, then, am I to tell whoever asks this question that this wasn't the case—that all of this didn't make her a Tiger Mother, that what cancels out the stereotype is that she has loved classical music all her life, that she has known its great beauty and wanted us to know it, too—when I cannot separate this answer from the fact that when you're an Asian person growing up in America, your choice to play and to love the violin is reduced, almost automatically, to the stereotype it is?

In physics, a symmetry is defined as the preservation of a system under a given transformation: the replacement of particles with their oppositely charged antiparticles, say, or the inversion of their orientation in space so that right is swapped with left and vice versa. When all the workings of the system remain unaltered in spite of that change, its symmetry is said to be preserved, its integrity maintained. If they do not, the system's continuity is ruptured in a process known as "symmetry breaking." Among the simplest examples of such transformations are space-translation symmetry, which shifts a system's position in space, and time-translation symmetry, which moves its operations to another place in time. (Galileo's experiments on falling bodies can be re-created today, more than four hundred years later, and the consistency of the results proves not only his original thesis— that acceleration due to gravity is the same for all objects, regardless of mass—but the constancy of physical laws across time, the immutability of gravity.) In instances of symmetry preservation, there is no discernible difference between before and after; something fundamental about the system's spatial and temporal position has changed, yet the physics of the system stays the same.

Is assimilation, then, the preservation of a symmetry or its breaking? On one hand, moving across the world in order to begin life anew necessitates undergoing a monumental translation in space and language and time, a transcontinental shift from there to here, then to now. You are required to change yourself, to break symmetry with the past and with the person you used to be; in many cases, perhaps, the desire for such a break motivates immigration itself. But what it's hard to appreciate until you've arrived in your new country, until it's too late, is that no matter what you do, no matter how hard you work or how successful you become, it doesn't really change how others see you—because the harder you try to transform yourself in order to fit in, the more you reveal yourself to be the outsider you always were. The very process of changing yourself, then, becomes an act of self-preservation:

You're just trying to prove that you belong, to make yourself acceptable to your new country so that you can survive inside of it.

More than anything, I think, my mother feared the time translation of her experience as an immigrant onto the lifetimes of her children: the possibility that we would have to endure the same uncertainty and degradation that she did, that her history would repeat itself. She wanted to break that symmetry at all costs. In this she has succeeded: I prepared to audition for Juilliard while she, at my age, had waited tables at a Chinese restaurant after school. The calluses on my hands are of a finer point than hers, formed over years spent pressing fingertips to violin strings, a far cry from the bleach-soaked, hard-scrubbing, cold-cracked years that her hands have endured.

Still, being humiliated for doing it this way has made her hesitate, has made her question herself. She seems shy now, sometimes, and halting; so conscious, always, of how she must be perceived, including by her own children. "I don't want you to be timid like me," she told me once, with a rueful laugh, and even though I reassured her and threw my arms around her, it broke my heart to hear her say it. As afraid as I am of what my music cost her, to question that choice is to deny her the right to have *made* a choice, to have a conviction and volition of her own about how her life ought to be. And yet can I deny that in defending her, I am really being defensive about myself and all the ways I prevailed upon her, took advantage of her sacrifice and was grateful, even happy, that she'd made it? When I tried miserably, haltingly, to tell her this, to get those feelings off my chest the year I woke her up almost every night to practice with me, she just smiled and shook her head and told me not to worry, that her job is to "launch the four of you—you know, to be the rocket booster, the thing that goes up with the rocket and propels it into space." What she didn't mention—yet implicit in her metaphor— is the fact that the rocket boosters, having given the last full measure of devotion at the upper limits of the atmosphere, must reverse their course and fall, spent, back to Earth.

—

"Try to give that phrase a little more shape. It'll help you stay in tempo, too, if you're thinking about the longer line."

She is right. The phrase sounds lost, wandering. It's close to 2:00 A.M. now. I am preparing for my audition at Juilliard, which is only a month away; the main piece is a concerto by Sibelius, and it's killing me. Parts of the score seem to me borderline unplayable, particularly the thunderous passage of double octaves at the end of the first movement, a long slide down the strings like a guttural wail- ing. Even the opening, which we are working on now—a single-voiced melody spinning out over a hollow and wind-picked landscape—is difficult to pin down. Practicing this piece, for this particular purpose, feels to me like a fight against invisible forces within the labyrinth of the self, against whose edges I risk bumping up unexpectedly in the dark, the boundaries of who I am and what I am capable of. Somehow, I can already feel that perhaps, for the first time, all my work and effort might not be enough. I play the phrase again, with more bow speed this time.

She smiles with warm and tired eyes. "Much better." I start to play it again, but then I hesitate and ask her something I have been longing to ask but have been too afraid to say till now: "When you quit, Uhmma—how did you know?"

She looks at me, studies me for a long moment. "I think you just know, if and when it *is* time. For you, the important thing is that you don't regret, and the important thing is that you choose."

All of a sudden I can't help it; a tear rolls down my cheek, then another and another. She stretches out her arms from the sofa. "Come here," she says, and I bury my face in her shoulder and bawl. "It's funny," she says after a minute, holding me, "this is just like how it was with my father."

He would sit up with her at night, too, Harabuji, reading as she finished her homework. He was sick when she was born and passed away a month after she turned thirteen. Their family immigrated to Colorado, in fact, so that he could be treated for tuberculosis at the lung hospital in Denver. "He loved classical music, too, you know," she says. "But it's more than that. Even though he died when I was so young, it felt like we spent a lifetime together. He and I lived all the mundane details of life in tandem—I was watering the lawn once with a garden hose, when I was really little, and I remember how he came over to help me, how gently he put this thumb over mine."

(Don't write it like a sob story, she said to me, years later, when I told her I was writing this book. She was worried I might make it sound as though her life has consisted only of hardship, or that she is ungrateful or resentful of the life she has been given. She says that she can never let herself feel as unlucky as she used to think she was; and when I ask her if she regrets marrying Dad, she always shakes her head fervently and says no. "I have the children I was meant to have," she says. "How blessed am I, to know the four of you, and to get to see what kind of people you'll become?" Our selves are equal parts our fate and our choice—but who can say what is one and not the other? And yet perhaps this is the fundamental difference between first- and second-generation immigrants, between sacrificial parent and prodigal child, the difference I am both afraid of and am somehow seeking. Our broken symmetry is that I, always, will feel as if I have the choice to walk away.)

"It's strange," she continues. Now she, too, is weeping. "You can be fifty, and you can be thirteen

. . ." She is sorry to burden me with her sad memories. She says she feels guilty that she had me so soon after her first baby died—my brother Alexander, who lived for only five days. She never could have been a Tiger Mother, not really, because all the rest of us had to do to make her happy was just wake up in the morning. "I couldn't hide it," she says, "how much I missed him. And then when you were born . . ." She shakes her head mournfully. "It was too great a burden to put on you, to love you so anxiously with too eager a heart."

Now, Uhmma, your memory is mine. Sometimes it felt, and feels still, that there is no separation between us—we think of the same word at the same time and our instincts are uncannily in sync. We knew, that year before I left for college, that it was the last year we would be together in the same house, living all the mundane details of life in tandem; we were afraid of what was coming but couldn't share this burden for fear of compounding it for each other. Those mornings when we struggled to keep each other awake, our shared will sustaining our combined effort, will be the memories I will tell my child. I feel it most acutely, now, remembering those moments of closeness that somehow laid bare the caverns of time and experience and sorrow between us: the shadow of that near symmetry between past and future, you and I;

the sense that we are somehow in sync yet perpetually out of phase in time. The fact that systems, people, memories can be symmetrically translated in time doesn't alter the fundamental asymmetry of time itself, whereby a known and immutable past plunges headlong into an uncertain future, one where we will be haunted both by what we have done, and what we have left undone.

Implicit in time's asymmetry, then, is the notion of becoming. The universe unspools itself toward a state of higher entropy; its edges fray, its dust is swept into corners, and this process of degradation and erosion is what separates the future from the past. We think of "becoming" as moving toward something final, evolving into a more perfect and more stable state over time. Yet, by proceeding forward in time, that very process must involve itself in the increasing disorder of the universe. When we seek to become something or someone else, to change our lives and leave the past behind, we necessarily abandon ourselves to entropy: We scatter old pieces of ourselves, willfully smudge our edges and make a mess of things, strive to break free of old symmetries that we feel can no longer contain us. Or, perhaps, that very instinct to change ourselves is a kind of preemptive embrace of the chaos we know is to come, a sign that we have already begun to spin out of control, that time is passing and taking us along with it and that soon nothing will be as it once was.

As I played that night in the library, my eyes, half closed, strayed from my music to the books on either side of the fireplace—your books, Uhmma, leaning against one another in the twin shelves. Nestled in the bottom corner of the right-hand shelf was your Nothing Book—a journal of bound colored paper containing poems and letters you wrote and folded and tucked away and have saved for forty years. I imagined you racing to your desk when you were seventeen, struck suddenly by an idea for a poem. You make those first daring marks on the blank sheet with shaky-fingered excitement—they seem at once a profanation and a solemn, sacred commencement. Later, you will read it again and tingle with modest embarrassment and shy pride, because it *is* a good poem. You were only seventeen and weren't quite sure what you meant, only that the words sounded right, especially the lines about the "bending moon," "the scopolamine truths," the "description to the point of self-erasure." Later, you will show it to your daughter, who will sense the shadow of your seventeen-year-old self somewhere between the words and her own seventeen-year-old heart. She will feel a selfish sadness that there is a part of you unknown to her and to which she is unknown, but it is because she loves you. She knows you haven't been able to write for a long time. There's always other, more immediate, more self-erasing work to be done.

Chaconne

Like the devils [that were once believed] to
inhabit humans, the [Bach] Chaconne must be
cast out of the body before the accursed can be
considered purified. That, however, is just what
does not happen. The Chaconne remains buried
within the violinist, a torment and a challenge
as long as he can tuck a fiddle under his chin.

— Irving Kolodin,
"Farewell to the Chaconne" (1985)

I want to begin the way the Chaconne is supposed
to begin: grave, momentous, sure of itself and of its
sorrow, that first D minor chord rending the solemn silence and yet consecrating something new,
setting in motion the iterative, underlying theme
that carries you toward the last bar in a kind of
canon, drawing from within itself a cry that is at
once savage and sacred, end and beginning.

And yet I cannot bring myself to play it. I stare
into the practice room mirror and notice a gray hair.
I examine it, yank it out, hunt for others. I leave
to get a drink of water. I scroll through Facebook.
It's been four months since I've touched my violin,

after almost two decades of daily, hours-long practice, and I am afraid to begin again, afraid of the sounds I might make, of what ugliness may come crawling out if I crack open that long a silence.

In many ways it had been four months of freedom: time for books that I'd long put off reading, walks along the Charles River while listening to Queen and Dire Straits, Ping-Pong tournaments at night when normally I would have stayed in the practice rooms till closing time at eleven, suddenly all this time to be filled up in the day. It was strange, not feeling oppressed by having to practice, and, in turn, feeling oppressed by *that* feeling. I was haunted, especially at first, by the opening up of time: I'd check my watch to calculate how much time I had left in the day to practice, before remembering that no, I didn't need to practice because I didn't play anymore. Now, facing the mirror in the dorm practice room, I feel in some ways as though no time has passed at all.

And yet time has caught up to me. I rub the tips of my left fingers with my thumb; their calluses have softened and shrunk. And my practice bruise—the rough purple spot on the left side of a violinist's neck that resembles a very ardent hickey—that badge of pride, won only after years of consistent practice, has faded, too. Four months might not sound like a lot, but when you are used to spending five to six hours a day in the practice room it adds up to a lot of empty time, a lot of lost progress. It hardly seems fair, but eighteen years of cultivated technique can deteriorate, if not entirely, then alarmingly fast, along with your hand strength; your fingers aren't as nimble or strong when you first return to playing, the way you can lose in a matter of weeks the muscle it took months to build up in the gym.

It is the Chaconne that has drawn me back. Four months into having quit for good, I'd started needing to play it. The piece is entirely solo and breathtakingly difficult—fifteen minutes long, with no breaks when an orchestra or piano might take over, no other parts to interact with, no one to save you from yourself if you mess up. Violinists consider it the most beautiful and unconquerable piece in our repertoire, and every serious player has their own interpretation of it. Thus to learn the Chaconne is a rite of passage, withheld by the teacher until the student is "ready," whatever that means. One usually learns it on the brink of turning from student to preprofessional—on leaving high school for conservatory, perhaps, or conservatory for graduate school and the professional auditions beyond. At any given point, wherever you are in your journey, the Chaconne represents the pinnacle of who you are and what you can do as a violinist—but you can always do better, right? In that way, you never *are* completely ready. You can practice it but not perfect it, start it but never finish it. Still, if I was going to quit, I didn't want to end without at least having learned it.

The Chaconne is the fifth and final movement of Johann Sebastian Bach's Partita No. 2 in
D minor, which itself is the second in his cycle of
six sonatas and partitas for solo violin. Bach composed the cycle—three *sonatas da chiesa* (church
sonatas), whose four movements alternate slow-
fast-slow-fast, and three partitas, which are suites
of dance movements—while he was Kapellmeister
at Anhalt-Köthen, a town in east-central Germany,
from 1717 to 1723. Bach worked as a church organist
and composer for most of his life, so much of what
he produced was religious music written for church
services. At one point in his career, he was writing
a new cantata every week. But he also composed
secular music, often as a study in how to master a
particular instrument. The violin solos are among
these, along with the suites for unaccompanied
cello and *The Well-Tempered Clavier* for piano (or
harpsichord, as it was then). It's widely believed that
Bach was in the middle of writing the violin solos
when his first wife, Maria Barbara, died. He was
vacationing with his employer in Carlsbad, more
than five hundred kilometers southwest of Köthen,
when she fell sick. Her illness was grave and sudden; there was no way to summon him home in
time. When Bach returned two months later, he
found her already buried in the Old Cemetery at
Köthen. In a frenzy of rage and grief, he composed
the Chaconne as a memorial and attached it to the
end of the second partita.

Musicologists have largely discredited this melodrama surrounding the Chaconne, if not debunked it entirely. Aside from the date 1720 on the manuscript of the violin solos, which was the year of Maria Barbara's death, there's really no evidence that Bach wrote the Chaconne as a memorial to her. But in some ways that hardly matters. The story persists in program notes for concerts, in online articles, in introductions to Bach's work. One ardent violinist, Trevor Ford, pleads in the online forum Quora, as though *not* knowing the story were an affront to the piece itself: "Here's the story, please do what you can to make violinists aware, as playing the Chaconne without the backstory is like trying to appreciate the Mona Lisa by touching it with your eyes closed." It's the story that violin teachers seem compelled to pass on to their students, which then becomes a memory so embedded in one's consciousness that the piece is inextricably connected to grief. But I think there is also something in the Chaconne itself that makes people want to believe the lore surrounding it is true.

As a musical form, a chaconne is simultaneously a dance in three-beat time and a series of continuous variations on a single harmonic theme, usually the same bass line repeated over and over again, which dictates the pattern of chords that anchor the variations to one another. Bach's Chaconne revolves in the conventional triple meter, with a

deep emphasis on each second beat; but there is
a terrible sorrow weighing it down, as though
the music itself is dancing a heavy-hearted waltz,
almost staggering with grief. It's longer than the
other four movements combined, almost a separate
piece in its musical and emotional scope. Yet shadows of each of the preceding movements dance and
flicker within its bar lines: a dotted rhythm like a
heavy sigh or step, like the one that opens the first
movement (Allemande) and which, condensed to
almost double speed, constitutes the main theme
of the Corrente; the descending chromatic bass
line that opens the Sarabande and is mirrored in
the Chaconne's first bars; a shimmering pattern of
alternating scales and arpeggios imported from the
Gigue. And yet the Chaconne is at the same time
entirely separate from these. It has always seemed
to me a lonely movement, riddled and reckoning
with the past.

There are other chaconnes by other composers—as a form it was especially popular during
the Baroque period—but Bach's is the most monumental and enduring. Yehudi Menuhin, one of the
great performers of the mid-twentieth century's
"golden age of violin playing," wrote in his autobi-
ography that the Chaconne is "the greatest structure for solo violin that exists." The contemporary
violinist Joshua Bell has called it "not just one of
the greatest pieces of music ever written, but one
of the greatest achievements of any man in history.

It's a spiritually powerful piece—emotionally powerful, structurally perfect." When the composer Johannes Brahms first heard it, in 1877, he wrote to Clara Schumann that

> [o]n one stave, for a small instrument, the man writes a whole world of the deepest thoughts and most powerful feelings. If I imagined that I could have created, even conceived the piece, I am quite certain that the excess of excitement and earth-shattering experience would have driven me out of my mind. If one doesn't have the greatest violinist around, then it is well the most beautiful pleasure to simply listen to its sound in one's mind.

Here's the thing—what happens when one *isn't* the greatest violinist around but wants more than just to listen to it in one's mind, or even to someone else's really good recording? I think most violinists feel some instinctive claim to the Chaconne, or at least a deep longing to play it and make it their own. After all, it's the pinnacle of our repertoire: It requires almost every traditional technique known to violinists; it consists not of one melodic line, but as many as four independent voices at one time, whose lines you can trace more or less from beginning to end. Sometimes it sounds as though the voices of an entire choir—soprano, alto, tenor, bass—are pouring in counterpoint out of the violin's f-holes. Within the Chaconne, a universe of feeling is bounded in a nutshell: many voices conflated into one, a lifetime of "deepest thoughts and powerful feelings" condensed into fifteen fleeting yet interminable minutes. I know of no piece more beautiful or more full of suffering.

It's just so damn hard. The primary technical difficulty, at least for me, lies in the execution of those contrapuntal (multivoiced) chords: the need to make each voice within the chord speak, to give each chord its proper weight while still maintaining a sense of horizontal flow, of keeping in time. But the technical difficulty is nothing compared to the emotional and physical stamina required just to get through those fifteen unrelenting minutes. You're alone, exposed, without respite; there's no stopping while another instrument plays, no relief until the end. You can practice it every day of your life and never express everything that it is capable of expressing. Still, practicing the Chaconne teaches you more about violin playing—and who you are as a violinist—than almost any other piece *because of* that very difficulty. It is a lifelong nemesis and bosom friend, the holy grail and the quest itself. For me, it was the last of the Bach violin solos: the only one I hadn't played, the missing piece.

I had tried learning the Chaconne once before, briefly, several years earlier, until a teacher told me I should stop playing it. It was the summer I was sixteen, and all I wanted was to be a violin soloist. I'd played most of the big pieces written for violin, the showpieces and concertos, tearing through them with a fierce and insatiable hunger, and I wanted to learn the Chaconne. That summer, I was attending the Meadowmount School of Music, an eight-week practice camp for classical-music students in rural upstate New York. All the best violinists, the ones I knew of, anyway, had gone there at some point, including my teacher Mr. Maurer; it was founded in 1944 by the legendary pedagogue Ivan Galamian, one of the primary figures (along with Menuhin) of the golden age of violinists. He is credited with developing a method of teaching—a system of scales and exercises in every key, an order in which pieces should be taught, his own editions of every famous concerto and of the Bach solos telling you exactly how to play them—that made learning the violin easier and more accessible. During its heyday in the late twentieth century, the best teachers taught at Meadowmount during the summers, keeping Galamian's tradition alive.

The camp consisted of a collection of dilapidated cabins at the top of a hill, alongside which ran a little dirt road that kept on for miles. You got shut inside your cabin for five hours a day—the counselors would keep vigil in the hall, walking around to each door and knocking if they heard you stop for too long—and you practiced the bejesus out of whatever you had been assigned. I was lucky because my window opened onto a view of the road and the countryside beyond. I'd open it while I practiced and gaze at the bottom of the hill, where the forest faded into a clearing with a farm surrounded by a little stone wall. The farm was within walking distance of the cabins, but it seemed almost a different world. In the mornings you woke up to the lowing of the cows.

My teacher for the summer was Mr. Maslow (not his real name), a man of imposing height with a long white mane of hair and glasses with thick black plastic rims. Behind them his eyes were mournful, distracted; he would often stare out the window of the lesson cabin while I played. At the end of my first lesson, my hands still shaking with fear, he told me that I was good but that if I wanted to even have a shot at being "a real violinist," I needed to go back to the beginning and relearn the basics, especially my bow hold. Kids were so good these days, the level of playing so high; there were so many techniques they could do with their flexible bow holds, and if I didn't change mine, there was really no way I could catch up. I left the lesson cabin fighting back tears. What hurt the most was the tired way in which he'd said it.

Over a lonely eight weeks, I worked to renovate my bow hold with a desperation I'd never felt before. I was used to the violin coming easily, to winning local competitions, to being good at it at home in Denver. Here, many of the kids during the school year attended the prep program at Juilliard, in New York City, on weekends and won competitions in Moscow and Brussels during the week. At Meadowmount, the very best students got to perform for the entire camp on Wednesday nights. The rest of us would get dressed up—there was a business-formal dress code just for sitting in the audience—and watch them make Paganini caprices look as easy as "Twinkle, Twinkle, Little Star." Humbled and afraid of being humbled further, I spent an extra three hours a day in my room practicing after the required five-hour shift was over, the mosquitos bumping lightly off the window screen, the forlorn exoskeletons of dead centipedes curled on the wooden sill. I changed my bow hold and spent those extra hours playing exercises with every bow stroke I could think of—legato, spiccato, martelé, at the tip and the frog, crossing strings and on each string by itself—to try to beat the new way into my brain, to take a hammer to a near lifetime of muscle memory and rebuild it the right way. That was the hardest part: not just the work of changing to something new, but also of undoing everything I already knew. As a respite from all the technical exercises, I started learning the Chaconne, hoping against hope that maybe Mr. Maslow would like it and I would get to play it at one of the concerts.

I never did, of course. At our last lesson, when the eight weeks were up, Mr. Maslow stopped me on my way out. He told me I'd done a good job fixing my bow hold but that it wasn't enough, that I should probably start focusing more on school since there wasn't really much of a chance that I could be a soloist, and most of the good orchestra jobs these days required soloist-level playing. Apparently it was one thing to fix your bow hold, but the fine-motor intricacies of left-hand position? Forget trying to undo and relearn that. And even if I did manage to fix my left hand—well, there were so many kids he'd taught who could just do it from the get-go. "You shouldn't be playing the Chaconne," he said, "it's too hard for you." I must have looked crestfallen, because then he added, more gently, "Look, you can always come back to it. It's one of those pieces that'll be with you your whole life." In a way he was right: It had haunted me all this time, the shadow of something left undone.

And that is why I am here, now, trying to start again: so that I can finally quit, finally exorcise those demons, finally satisfy those ghosts and lay them to rest. I didn't stop playing after that summer at Meadowmount; if anything, I practiced harder. *I'll show you, Maslow,* I thought. I won more competitions, became the concertmaster of the youth symphony, performed concertos with orchestras all over Colorado. Still, I knew deep down that it would never be enough. All the practicing—the mind-numbing repetitions, the bloody fingernails, the brutally late nights—was either a way of convincing myself it would all be worth it or punishing myself for the fact that it wouldn't, I'm not sure which.

It was only after my father left, four years after that summer, that I suddenly wanted to let go, or finally felt like I could. He had always hated the music, restricting when and where I could practice and forbidding any singing and even whistling in the house. I can count on one hand the number of performances he attended in the two decades I played; the few times he did show up, I looked out into the audience and could tell exactly where he was sitting because of the blue light radiating upward from his phone. Perhaps it was the despair of never being good enough—for the violin or for him—which was actualized by his leaving, brought to a head by it. This time I couldn't convince myself things would be fine if only I worked harder; but in a way that, too, was its own kind of relief. Why keep on trying to love something that doesn't love you back? If anything, Dad's leaving gave me an excuse for not having to try so hard anymore.

Learning the Chaconne this time, I'm not working *toward* something, exactly. There's not a concert or a master class coming up toward which to direct my practice, or as a reward *for* all the practice. No, this time I am practicing to quit. And I need to end with the Chaconne.

And so back to the beginning. It's one D minor chord; it's not that difficult; I can feel the shadow of it in my fingertips. But I can't bring myself to draw the bow. It's like when you want to tell someone how you feel but don't quite have the words, and you swallow into silence because you are afraid of what you might say, of how you might dismay and astonish yourself.

—

Bach is a master of self-effacement. Not that his music itself is meek, far from it; there's an assuredness to its sound that derives from the boldness and clarity of its harmonic patterns.* Bach shaped Western tonality as we know it, and as such we owe much of our modern sense of tension and release (and thus emotion) in music—which chords yearn toward one another, which back away, which are dark or light—to him. Nor was he himself timid, based on what little we know of his character: He was often getting into scrapes and being reprimanded by the churches that employed him, including for overstaying a leave by three months, dueling

---

* He also often slipped his musical signature—the note sequence Bb - A - C - B♮ (in German, Bb is notated as simply B and B♮ as H, so B-A-C-H)—into thematic material, though for me this doesn't change the absence of directed emotional expressivity in his music. He is present but transfigured, a name distilled into four notes for the performer to shape and interpret as they will.

with a church bassoonist who set upon him with a walking stick after Bach insulted his performance, and inviting a "strange maiden" to "make music" in the church's organ loft. No, Bach's music is self-effacing because it contains so little trace of *him*. He doesn't micromanage the performer's interpretation: rarely, if ever, does he specify dynamics, articulation, bow stroke, timing in his scores. He leaves all of these for the performer to decide.

Such restraint is not unusual for composers of the Baroque era, who tended to mark less in their scores because most performances, even of prewritten pieces, were improvised to some degree. Players would add trills and other ornamentation to their solo lines, sometimes even small cadenzas, which they made up on the spot. Composers, in turn, relied on the assumption that whoever was performing would know the conventions of how to execute the music and how to improvise within those conventions. In later periods, by contrast, composers became more precise and demanding about how they wanted their pieces interpreted. Beethoven, of the late Classical/early Romantic period, long-haired and wild-eyed, is famous for the specificity of his dynamics and the abrupt celerity with which his music shifts from loud to soft: a forte on one beat, a piano on the next, yoked together in a violent chiaroscuro of sound. His style matched the caprice of his personality, the suddenness of his oscillations between rage and tenderness.

There's a different quality to Bach's music that sets him apart from the rest of the Western canon, even from other Baroque composers. Maybe *self-effacement* isn't exactly the right word, because he *is* present in his music, his style distinctive. It's more a quality of restraint, as though he's held himself back from full self-assertion. His music is just not *about* him, somehow. Perhaps this is because of the context in which he wrote for most of his life, as a composer for the liturgy, and his deep faith in God. He signed all of his religious compositions, approximately a thousand of them, "SDG": *Soli Deo gloria*, "to God alone the glory." The way God is glorified through prayer—not by words of worship only, but by the very act of kneeling before Him—*that's* how Bach wrote. He removed his ego from his music so that he might make of that music a worthy offering.

This deep humility pervades even his secular compositions. It manifests itself, musically, as a preoccupation with structure and form rather than overt expressivity. Bach wrote most of his compositions in counterpoint—that is, with a multiplicity of simultaneous independent lines, so that no one voice is privileged too long over the others. Instead, they are constantly in argument and dialogue. He didn't write melodies—which inherently highlight one voice against the backdrop of the accompanying parts—but themes, snippets of phrases or harmonic movements that can be deconstructed and reconstructed, contracted and augmented, layered on top of one another to build the altar on which he worships God, and on which he allows you, the performer, to offer yourself. Making sense of these themes so that the entire structure is internally justified, giving all the voices their due weight, and finding the feeling in their interplay, is the work of the performer. You are doing the musical carpentry, the humble work of building those structures, right along with Bach. It's difficult but not flashy; there's not the bombast of execution that comes with a violin concerto, its flying bow strokes and daredevil runs, the excitement of which comes as much from the player's ability to execute them as from the music itself. Even in a concerto's slow, melodic movements, the player is tasked with finding the elusive middle ground between self-expression and what the composer wanted to say. With Bach, there is little difference between the two, because his music *is* feeling itself. There is nothing to cover it, nowhere to hide, nothing to mitigate its ecstasy or its suffering: *de profundis clamavi ad te Domine*, out of the depths I cry unto you, O Lord. Bach strips away the ego of both composer and performer, with all its defenses and desires, in order to lay bare pure feeling: a sin confessed after a long silence, a head bowed in prayer.

At Meadowmount a girl named Tegan, who lived across the hall from me, was also playing the Chaconne. We'd often practice it at the same time; sometimes we played in a kind of unintended canon, two solitary voices echoing each other. We talked about how hard it was to craft an interpretation of the Chaconne, how to make sense of all those variations. But whereas I felt lost just trying to get the notes, she had a way forward with it, a vision and a way in: She thought the Chaconne represented the five stages of grief, the way you move through time from denial to anger to bargaining to depression to acceptance after you lose someone you love.

Tegan's interpretation has always stuck with me, and I thought of it immediately when I flipped again, years later, in my Bach book to the Chaconne. "Stages of grief," I'd written in my careful teenage handwriting, in the top corner on the first page. Now I wonder if those stages can be so clearly defined, or if grief can be divided into stages at all. *Stages* implies a progress through time, gives the illusion of linearity—but this is not my experience of grief. Even when I listen all the way through to the end of the Chaconne, I don't have any sense of having worked through the grief it makes me feel. The sadness is still there, as raw as it ever was. What I *do* have, or have had in that moment, is a complete experience (perhaps even embrace) of the feeling in all its myriad forms, its painful variations. I have let myself feel; I have let myself remember.

The Chaconne ends the way it begins, with the same lamentation, the eight original thematic bars that rend the silence, a bellow, a gut-cry, a *de profundis*. That simultaneity of end and beginning gives the impression, at least to me, that the entire Chaconne has unfolded within a single moment. The entire piece, which is contained within the statement and restatement of the theme, is a meditation on that feeling, sixty-four variations on the memory of those opening bars. The variations abide by slightly different chord progressions but retain the same circular shape; each ends the way it began, with a D minor sonority, leading seamlessly into the next variation in a perfect ellipse of end and beginning. They take the form not of linear stages but iterative, circular variations, different feelings and memories buried within one another. Within each circle is contained a world of memory and sorrow, as though the moment has opened wide, the waves of time expanded, their oscillation slowed.

Form, in music, is inherently temporal. It gives some shape to time, or at least designates the pace and manner at which we move through a particular piece. Where do we fare forward or cycle back; which moments expand, and which contract? Likewise, memory—that most universal and yet individual of temporal structures—lends form and shape to experience in biographical time. We inhabit simultaneous, concentric timescales: the time line of the past coiled within the immediacy of the present moment unfolding. Memory creates a metonymic congruence between them, melding past with present in such a way that our former selves move forward with us in time. But grief ruptures that momentum. The dam breaks; those currents converge into an eddy of memory, desire, and regret, an almost inescapable, endless circling back into what once was, what has been. This is what Bach understood, and made manifest in the Chaconne—all the gravitational aspects of grief, which you experience perpetually in cycle and flashback and variation. You don't move on from loss so much as move away, further out in time. But in a sudden instant you can remember everything again; the past comes alive, and an entire chaconne is unleashed within the emotional arrest of that moment, a spiral of related memories and buried feeling. In this way, the Chaconne—enclosed by the same thought, the same phrase that is both end and beginning, that feeling of loss that sends you spiraling down the wormhole of memory only to arrive at itself—enacts the way memory can expand a moment in time. To grieve is to experience these painfully expanded moments over and over again, often without warning . . . to think you've gotten away from the past only to awaken to it, to get the wind knocked out of you all over again, to feel the omnipresence of that loss.

During one lesson halfway through the eight weeks at Meadowmount, Mr. Maslow stopped me about thirty seconds into the Chaconne. I had just finished the opening theme, the famous eight bars that somehow touch upon four metal strings the weight of all human suffering. I guessed from his face that I hadn't played them particularly well, or well enough. "Look," said Maslow, "look, it's all wrong." He sighed and gazed out the window of his teaching cabin. It was bright midmorning; far away a tiny speck of a farmer was urging his cows gently across the pasture. Mr. Maslow seemed to change his mind about something and looked back at me.

"Do you know the story of this piece?" he asked. His voice sounded very weary. I nodded my head yes; Mr. Maurer had told it to me before I left. "Well, it bears repeating," Maslow replied, and he launched into the tale of Maria Barbara Bach. It took him a while to tell the story; I had the vague sense that he was trying to eat up lesson time. My fingers got sort of stiff and clammy and I had to keep wiping them on my shirt, in case he had me play again.

"But that's not the only story, you know. Some people think—and I'm inclined to believe this—that Bach wrote the whole cycle of sonatas and partitas as a representation of Christ's life. He was a very religious man, you know. And the Chaconne is where Christ gets crucified—the crux of the cycle, as it were. It's the longest movement in the whole cycle, with the biggest climax. It's also the end of the minor keys—the third sonata and third partita, which come after the D minor, are the only ones in major keys. The whole cycle kind of gets resurrected. But this is the low point."

I thought of the Crucifixion scene in the stained

glass at St. John's, the cathedral our family occa-
sionally went to in Denver (mostly on Christmas
and Easter, and mostly as a formality; Dad would
joke about absolving ourselves of a year's weight of
sin on those two days, though I never walked out
feeling that much lighter). I used to be afraid of the
images in the grim stained glass, the Crucifixion in
particular; I almost couldn't bear to look head-on at
the terrible contorted faces at the foot of the cross,
the blood spurting out of the slit in Christ's side.
The lead framings seemed like black ropes binding the figures' bodies. The cathedral itself held a
kind of morbid fascination, the moody lighting and
the musty candle smell, the somberness, the stone
saints' grisly ecstasy. It was hard to avoid looking
at the stained glass when you went up to the altar
for Communion; when I was little, walking up the
aisle with my father, I would look just long enough
to catch sight of it and then bury my face in my
father's side.

I still think of that stained glass whenever I hear
the Chaconne, perhaps because it's so encoded in
my memory of my first learning of that piece with
Mr. Maslow. But it's hard, now, to disaggregate that
memory from the memories that followed: how it
felt to go back to St. John's without Dad for the
first time; not hearing his deep bass voice recite
the Nicene Creed, which mysteriously he could do
from memory even though he wasn't religious and
never had been; not trying to stifle a laugh as he

played "the watch game," catching a little circle of blue light from the stained glass on the face of his watch and making it dance on the ceiling. He hated sitting through the homily; in that way he was almost like a child. When my siblings and I were really little, he'd use us as an excuse to get out of the pew and walk around the back of the church to pass the time. We'd return, though, for the hymns at the end of the service, which the congregation got to sing with the choir: "Hark the Herald Angels Sing" on Christmas, "He Is Risen" on Easter. Dad loved these—why, I never knew. I always found it strange that he liked the hymns so much when we weren't allowed to sing at home. When I was little it seemed miraculous to hear him sing and to sing beside him. I remember rising to sing on that first Christmas without him and not being able to get the words out. Listening to the flow of the music around and past me, I felt like a stone stuck in the stream of time. I remember looking up at the altar and the stained glass, at all the anonymous heads around me—some bowed in prayer, others raised in song—and feeling dazed, almost, taken out of time; gazing around in bewildered sorrow, because nothing was different and everything had changed.

—

After twenty minutes of failing to start the Chaconne, I chicken out and decide to play scales, a more productive way of stalling. I start off with octave exercises, shifting one octave up each string on each finger, one by one. I collect impressions and make mental notes as I go, testing to see if I still have that sixth sense that comes with steady practice, that intuitive knowledge of the invisible notch on the fingerboard where each note locks in. A little wobbly at first, but it comes back. Left wrist flaring up slightly. The pain is an old reminder; the twinge comes back when I haven't played in a while and try to start up again, as though wagging its finger at me for having slacked off or stayed away too long. Ironic that it should have come from playing too *much* in the first place.

When I was fourteen, having just decided for real that I wanted to be a violinist, a few months of earnest overpracticing and bad technique stretched a ligament in my left wrist to a near breaking point. Then the same thing happened on the right (my bow hold was not as relaxed as I'd thought). Mr. Maurer took me off his regimen of difficult études and concertos with all the fancy bowing and high shifts. For six months all I played was Bach.

They were six months in which I barely felt like myself. I could only play for about ten minutes at a time before my hands felt weak. As a result I hardly knew what to do with my time. Still, whenever I could play, I played the sonatas and partitas. They're not show-offy the way concertos or Paganini caprices are; they don't require the same technical bombast, the high shifts and lightning-fast runs, and therefore didn't strain my hands as much. They kept me company, tethered me to myself. I grew to know them better and love them more than any other pieces I'd ever played. I learned all of them except the Chaconne.

When you're starting out on the violin, you're told that if you just work hard enough, you can make it. That promise becomes a kind of desperate creed, the one thing you can hold on to when you start to realize that you'll never be as good as you wish you could be. I tell myself that my experience at Meadowmount shook that faith, but maybe that's what happens anyway when you get older and realize it's all a losing battle. You just don't want to have to believe anymore.

Now, facing myself in the practice room mirror, I'm trying to begin all over again but without the same faith. Idiot, I think, why did you want to quit so much? Isn't it really because you didn't want to quit at all? In fact, you were afraid of it, afraid of having to stop like you had to when you were fourteen and couldn't play because your hands weren't strong enough, except that this time you would have to stop because *you* weren't strong enough. Isn't that what you have to accept now— that it won't be your career, that it won't be part of your life the way you'd thought or hoped? Yes, all of that you have to come to terms with. . . . But you also have to accept the opposite, somehow: that it will always be a part of you, that you'll never be able to quit and have that be that. You'll never be able to free yourself from how much you love it, or from the belief—indoctrinated by all those years of devoted practice and practiced devotion—that, if you try hard enough, you can still be the violinist you thought you would be.

I returned from Meadowmount hating the violin. And I've hated it ever since, if only because that's easier than still loving it. When my dad left, he wrote in a court testimonial during custody proceedings that I was "maladaptive" for practicing so much. He didn't know that I hated the violin, that I hated it because of all the time it had cost me with my brothers and my sister, with my mom and with him; time I gave to the violin instead, time I can't get back, especially now that we aren't all together anymore. And yet at the same time, the violin embodies and expresses all that I am and have been. When I play it's a way of inhabiting again, even for a moment, the person I once was.

During my sophomore year of college, shortly before I stopped playing, I went home to Denver and performed a few movements of Bach for a recital, a leftover requirement from a scholarship I'd won my last year of high school. Mr. Maurer was there; he came up afterward to give me his polite yet paternal hug. He was nothing like Mr. Maslow. He made no pronouncements about whether a student would succeed or not, what kind of career they would have (or not). Even though he was a prodigy himself, able to play the violin seemingly without struggle, he believed that as long as you practiced, you could make it. If you didn't, well, then the odds were against you. I think he was happy and vaguely surprised to see that I was still playing, still going at it, still beating my head against the same wall. During lessons, he used to hold the score of whatever piece I was playing and mark it as I ran through, inscribing tiny cursive *X*s below the parts where I'd messed up or needed to improve. When I fixed something from the week before, that *X* got circled, neatly, with his black number-two pencil which never lost its sharpness.

"So what are you thinking for after college, Natalie? Music graduate school?"

"Yes," I croaked, although nothing could have been further from the truth.

"And where do you want to go?"

"Um, Juilliard?" I hadn't wanted to go any-where near the "Jailyard" since I'd visited it in high school and confirmed that it was, in fact, a jail yard. Or at least that I would find it so.

Mr. Maurer beamed the way he used to when he could tell I'd practiced hard and he'd circled all the *X*s and I'd gotten everything right.

"You just can't keep away from that violin, can you," he smiled.

"No," I replied. And it's true: I can't, no matter how much I want to, no matter how hard I try.

The hall connecting the practice rooms is dark. It's 10:30 P.M., almost closing time. I am just about to pack up and go home when I remember, in a flash, something else Mr. Maslow told me at Meadowmount all those years ago. "You don't always have to start at the beginning," he'd said. He was annoyed with the way I'd been practicing, because the beginnings of pieces were always so much better than the middle sections and the endings; between lessons I'd chisel obsessively away at the openings and then run out of time to work on the other parts.

In the middle of the Chaconne, there is a pause that lasts for less than the space of a breath and yet, somehow, for an eternity. The roiling purple darkness of D minor dissipates, and out of the silence begins a single D major chord, barely a touch to the strings, a breath of bright wind. The variations that it sets in motion play upon the same theme as before, but the surrounding harmonies that fill in its shape are in D major. If D minor is darkness, then D major is light; it shares the minor's grandeur but not its sadness. It is radiant, ebullient, sparkling, full of life.

The section is one long crescendo toward ecstasy, full of open strings, where you don't put any fingers down and just bow, letting the strings ring out in their full and elemental clarity. Violinistically, it's a delight to play: The open strings set your entire violin trembling, so that you can feel the wood itself ringing against your neck and shoulder as you bow. When I was learning the Chaconne at Meadowmount, this was the one part that didn't seem so hard, that made sense, that felt free. I can feel it now, remembering—that quickening overtakes you: You and your violin are one, intensely and ecstatically present. Bach adds another iterated element, a trinity of repeated notes—either A or D—that sound like the striking of a bell. They create a kind of ellipse between the end of each phrase and the beginning of the next, linking and extending them into one continuous moment; they are alpha and omega, beginning and end, and their persistent chiming announces, over and over again, the present moment. To play them you have to traverse the open strings of the violin, from high to low, sounding the depths of the instrument and the moment. The repeated notes begin small and sweet and then increase in their resonance and warmth, until the notes are ringing out with a joy that defies all containment, a bright effusion, a shout from the mountaintops. You can't help but feel some sacred presence, there, in the midst of grief; the music continues building and rising until it can no longer contain itself, and you feel the light that is spilling forth, the joy of being delivered from yourself. With each iteration the feeling grows stronger, the conviction deeper, the present moment freer of the past.

I'd forgotten the beauty of the D major section,

the way everything sounds present, everything feels alive. It's the one moment of respite from memory in the entire piece, the way you can be taken out of grief, even momentarily, by something beautiful: the sight of a green hill after rain, the blue light from a stained-glass window, the voice of a violin. Maybe this is where I can start, how I can find my way back in: not by going back to the beginning, to beat my head against the familiar discouragement and despair, but to the hope for some kind of grace as I cycle back in the perpetual chaconne of memory, a negotiation and reconciliation leading to some moments when just playing itself will be enough.

And so I find the notch of the D major chord with my left hand, place my bow on the strings, and feel forward for the notes to come.

The Still Point
of the Turning World

At the still point of the turning world.
Neither flesh nor fleshless;
Neither from nor towards; at the still
point, there the dance is . . .

—T. S. Eliot, "Burnt Norton"

Hurrying to the Quad in the cold, almost late, I was overtaken by a man walking swiftly and determinedly, exhaling white gusts into the November evening. I wondered if perhaps he was Thomas but couldn't get a good look, and, feeling suddenly shy, I didn't want to take a chance and introduce myself and be wrong. Only after about five minutes of following him at a semi-creepy distance did I determine that, yes, he was indeed Thomas. He is a tall man with a lively gait; this particular evening he carried a green backpack slung over his right shoulder and swung his left arm powerfully yet elegantly as he walked. A few blocks from the Quad, he stopped in the middle of the sidewalk to take a picture of a building across the street. When I arrived at the same spot I saw what, I imagined, had arrested him:

a man playing a piano at the window of a warmly lit apartment whose walls were covered from floor to ceiling with books. The man's lips moved as he sang to himself, but I could hear no sound.

The penthouse of the Quad's student organization center has a beautiful suite with a dance floor in the middle and bright wood-paneled walls. Twelve other people (seven women, five men) milled about inside in various states of dress, some wearing workout clothes or, having come straight from work or class, with dress shirts untucked; others were in silk skirts and dancing shoes. In a corner, Thomas was preparing the music on his laptop and talking to a beautiful woman with a swishy wine-colored skirt and a long braid down her back. People who weren't in dancing shoes had lined up their sneakers and flats by the door; the room smelled faintly of feet. All of us were there to dance tango.

Or, more specifically, to *learn* to dance tango. It was 7:00 P.M. and we were attending the beginner class of the college Argentine Tango Society, which convened every Monday during the school year. Thomas Wisniewski, then a graduate student in comparative literature, had founded the society in 2011; he taught this class and an intermediate-advanced class afterward, along with Silvana Brizuela (the lady in the wine-colored skirt), a professional dancer from Buenos Aires who taught and performed in Boston. They had taught over eight hundred people how to tango since the society's inception.

This particular evening marked ten weeks into the fall 2018 series; the class was working up to a final *milonga*—in Thomas's words, a "big tango party"— in December. The music started, a slow, melancholy tango full of sighs, played by an *orquesta típica** on a crackly record, and people began pairing off and practicing the techniques from last week. There was still a lot of awkwardness, a lot of uncertainty and tentative movements, but everyone was friendly and game. As they warmed up in pairs you could see the halting shadow of a dance start to emerge.

I was there due to a combination of compulsion and coincidence. The compulsion—to play tango music—was one I'd had for four years by then, ever since my high school string quartet, in our last year together, randomly flipped to an arrangement of Carlos Gardel's "Por una Cabeza" in our gig book and decided to play it. "Por una Cabeza" is one of the most famous and recognizable tangos of all time, and many a layman's introduction to the genre (like mine). Al Pacino and Gabrielle Anwar dance to it in the movie *Scent of a Woman*, in that famous scene where a blind Pacino leads Anwar spontaneously across a dance floor with both tenderness and a kind of savagery. After that introduction I began playing all the tango music I could

* A traditional tango orchestra or band of eight to twelve musicians, usually consisting of strings, piano, and bandoneon.

find, although there was still something missing. Years later, I realized that if I was going to *really* learn tango, inevitably I would have to summon the courage to dance.

The coincidence was that I already knew Thomas. We'd met only once, two years before, through my Shakespeare professor, who happened to be Thomas's dissertation adviser. At that point in college, having sunk almost twenty years into trying to be a violinist and yet feeling rather glum about my career prospects, I was getting ready to call it quits. My professor, aware of my doubts, connected me to Thomas, a professional-level saxophonist who was studying prose rhythms in literature. Thomas reassured me that I didn't have to choose one thing over the other, that he'd had the same struggle once and had figured out a way to do both. Later, when I was searching for a tango class in Boston, I recognized him in his profile on the Tango Society's web page.

Thomas introduced me to Silvana, who has warm eyes and a mischievous smile, and then I joined the others on the floor. I began to feel the sweaty anxiety of having never done this before and of being the only new one, coupled with the awkwardness of having to find a partner, but then I was swept along as Thomas beckoned and everyone filed to the perimeter of the dance floor.

Thomas and Silvana stood at the center, facing each other. "Today we are going to learn the most important step in tango," Thomas said. The class had already learned some basic moves: *la caminada*, the tango walk, and *el ocho*, a figure-eight step pattern done in place. And they had learned how to hold each other in *el abrazo*, the embrace of tango partners that is the dance's heart and that encloses the ember of its fire and its sadness. But they weren't really *dancing* yet. "This step is called *el giro*," Thomas continued, "the turn. One partner revolves around the other—or both around each other, at the same time. Once you learn this, all of tango will open up to you. In fact, once you learn this, you can start to improvise."

Improvise? My heart seized up. I'd thought they were going to teach us a sequence of moves, a set pattern that would loop over and over again, like with the fox-trot or the waltz, where you know where you are as long as you keep repeating the same steps. I hadn't realized that about tango—that the dance is made up on the spot. All the tangos I had watched seemed choreographed down to the last flourish, the last lingering glide of a heeled foot across the floor, so connected were the couples, so silently and flawlessly in sync.

Silvana and Thomas demonstrated *el giro*. At first they danced without touching: Thomas turned slowly in place, his feet touching at the heels and pivoting one after the other, while Silvana executed the steps of *el giro*, revolving around him like the hands of a strange majestic clock. Then suddenly they joined together and began whirling across the floor, combining the turn with the tango walk and the *ochos*, which the class already knew how to do. "Now," Thomas said, "we're *really* improvising." Without warning, he spun Silvana into a series of rapid-fire *giros* and *ochos*. We all watched her with our mouths open. When they stopped and Silvana saw us, she smiled wryly, anticipating everyone's question. "How do I know?" She touched Thomas's chest. "I follow the GPS."

That's Silvana's own term, the *GPS*: a specific point just below the hollow of your partner's throat, toward which you are supposed to focus all your energy and from which you draw your partner's energy, as though from a well of aura and light. You're *not* supposed to look at your or your partner's feet—which is certainly the temptation, especially when you are new and embarrassed and afraid of messing up and constantly averting your eyes from your partner's, because looking anywhere else is infinitely more bearable while you are in that terrible breathtaking embrace. Instead, you focus with all your might toward that hollow, that still point which remains a center of gravity as the rest of you revolves. "In the close embrace you can feel everything," Thomas says, and thus anticipate everything: It's almost as though you know what your partner is going to do before they do it. In a way, then, the distinction between leader and follower melts away. You can only follow by anticipating, which is perhaps its own kind of pre-conscious leading.

To dance tango with a stranger is almost unbearably intimate. I practiced *el giro* with a woman named Ana, a grad student in electrical engineering, and then Alej, who works at Mass General. Alej threw a coin on the floor for us to dance around while we drilled *el giro*, to create a kind of still point, a locus around which we could turn. At one point, Thomas told the followers to reach out and "actually touch the leader's GPS, so you can learn to sense the signals"; I had to put my hands on Alej's chest after having known him for about five minutes. It was embarrassing—my palms, to my horror, left light sweat spots on his shirt—but I got a sense of how intense the *abrazo* is, felt the fear and trembling of that close encounter. And I sensed, too, how responsive the mind and body could be when in such proximity to another human being, if that initial embarrassment could be overcome; how it would be easy—instinctive, almost—to know not only what your partner is going to do before they do it, but also to be certain that *they* know what *you* are going to do, and thus to keep with them in time. Turning over and over around the coin, syncing our steps and our sense of *when* to step, Alej and I started to get it: a dizzy kind of entrainment, but entrainment nonetheless.

It fell apart immediately, of course, as soon as Thomas told us to try combining the *giro* with other moves. Each of us was trying and failing to follow our partner's GPS, and, for that matter, to send out strong-enough signals from our *own* GPS. There were people turning every which way and tripping over one another. Thomas gave a knowing smile as he looked out over the tangle of hapless pairs. "The more you dance, the more this connection will just generate movement. It will produce steps. *That* is improvisation. It's like learning to play jazz."

Forty-six years in the past and over three thousand miles away, two photons were performing the dance of improvised time. The year was 1972, and at the Lawrence Berkeley National Laboratory in Berkeley, California, John Clauser and Stuart Freedman had just produced the first experimental verification of quantum entanglement. Entanglement—as theorized in 1964 by the Irish physicist John Stewart Bell—is the theory that quantum particles (particles smaller than atoms) can affect one another's behavior without acting on one another directly. Till then, mainstream physicists maintained that particulate behavior had to obey the classical laws of locality, by which objects can be influenced only by events in their immediate environments—because in Einsteinian terms, no information can travel between physical bodies faster than the speed of light. In other words, the particles would have to act on one another by applying force or entering one another's magnetic field, et cetera, for one to affect the properties of the other. Clauser and Freedman showed that this wasn't the case: For a reason they couldn't explain, some of the photons in their experiment were able to sync their polarizations—the direction of their vibrating electrical fields—instantaneously, without communicating with one another in any traditionally explicable sense.

As physicists have replicated Clauser and Freedman's results over and over, the existence of some nonlocal connection between quantum particles has become virtually impossible to deny. Today, some physicists believe that any given particle "is entangled with many particles far outside our horizon." Thus, much of quantum behavior remains unobservable and unknowable to us. But when two "directly entangled" particles *are* isolated in an experiment, something magical, miraculous, and downright spooky happens: Passing one entangled photon through a polarizing filter, which gives it either a horizontal or vertical polarization, *immediately* polarizes the other in the same direction, even though that second particle is nowhere near the polarizer—and even if it is nowhere near the other particle. Recently, a team at MIT demonstrated that entanglement can act across vast swaths of space-time, between particles that are billions of light-years apart. Theoretically, the connection is both infinite and instantaneous. No matter how far apart the particles are in either time or space, those distances can be folded into a simultaneity in which the two particles act as though they are one. And while it is understood that entangled particles are produced constantly by natural processes, and can be tailor-made by physicists in labs, no one knows the true nature of their connection itself.* The best way that physicists have of describing it, the one that crops up in myriad videos and journal articles and polemical rants in online physics forums, is that the particles somehow "just know."

----

* One current and promising theory, posited by Juan Maldacena and Leonard Susskind in 2013, is that entangled particles are connected by wormholes, theoretical shortcuts through space-time that bridge one point directly with another. Under general relativity, it is possible for two black holes, distant from one another in space-time, to be linked directly by a wormhole, a tunnel connecting their interiors. Maldacena and Susskind propose that this wormhole is, in fact, equivalent to the entanglement of the two black holes. Their conjecture's name—"ER=EPR"—derives from two papers coauthored by Einstein in 1935, the first of which discovered wormholes between black holes, or Einstein-Rosen (ER) bridges, and the second of which studied "spooky action at a distance" between entangled particles called Einstein-Podolsky-Rosen (EPR) pairs. Maldacena and Susskind go on to suggest that "similar bridges might be present for more general entangled states"—not on the scale of black holes alone, but between any entangled particles, anywhere in space-time. The less powerful the particles' entanglement, the more quantum the wormhole that connects them. See "Cool horizons for entangled black holes," arxiv.org/abs/1306.0533.

This is the quantum-physical concept of coincidence: the unpredictable synchronicity of two beings in time. It seems to me that in tango, and perhaps in all instances of simultaneous improvisation, a similar kind of coincidence is at play. Of course the dancers don't dance at a distance, and the jury is still out on whether entanglement can be extrapolated from the quantum physical to the human and biological, but you can't escape the feeling that there must exist some kind of instantaneous, unconscious connection between improvising partners. Entanglement theory holds that before the particles are polarized, whether they will take on a vertical or horizontal polarization is equally probable. In other words, until the moment that one of them passes through the filters, the entangled pair's polarization is simultaneously vertical and horizontal, the way Schrödinger's cat is both dead and alive until you open the box. The instant one of them passes through the filter, its polarization changes; and the other changes with it, as though it always knew in which direction its partner was destined to vibrate. In tango, likewise, you have to hold all the possibilities for each next move in your mind, at every moment, and yet in each moment you know exactly which step to take. If nothing else, tango ought to join the pantheon of metaphors for that quantum connection—describable, at least for now, in figurative terms only—which are as varied as they are numerous: the intuition shared by a pair of twins;

the Covenant Between the Parts in Genesis; an umbilical cord; a mind-reading, instantaneous GPS.

Once, Thomas and Silvana had us drill *el giro* without touching, practicing the footwork only. Some partners, out of instinct, kept trying to hold each other by the arms. Thomas shut it down. "Stop, stop, everyone. Pedagogical intervention!" He made all of us step apart and do the exercise individually, because obviously we could not handle it in pairs. "No hands! I mean it! These are *drills*. Silvana never knows when I want her to stop turning until she *knows*—not because we're touching. The hands help, but the feeling comes first. *That's* what you have to practice." It's essentially an exercise in the principle of nonlocality, as applied to tango: Somehow, without applying any force or having any physical contact with your dance partner, you match each other's movements through instinct and intuition. There isn't time for the leader to give a cue and then for the follower to pick up on it and respond and for both of them to execute it together. The only way to keep the dance flowing in time is for each partner to intuit how the other will move, even if you don't know exactly what you are intuiting: communion without direct communication, intimacy without knowledge; the simultaneous leaping of entangled minds.

The simultaneity in tango begins even before the dance itself, with an invitation from one dancer to another. When I interviewed Thomas one rainy afternoon in December 2018, he noted how the invitation itself sets the tone of the entire *tanda*, the set of tangos that two people dance together at a *milonga* before switching to new partners. It's not the traditional ballroom invitation, a sweeping bow and an ostentatious "May I have this dance?" but one that is knowing and wordless and often simultaneous. One person, usually the man (if the couple is heterosexual), will look at the other while both are waiting to dance, single her out with his gaze. If she returns his glance, he nods at her; if she accepts the invitation, she nods back and they meet on the dance floor. That invitation— *la mirada y cabeceo*, the look and the nod—establishes the connection between partners, the chemistry that will spark their *tanda* and make the dance unique to that couple while it lasts. Thomas believes the system was developed in order to "make rejection invisible," at least to the larger group. As such, there is no accepting out of guilt or pity or awkwardness; indeed, *la mirada y cabeceo* is accepted only if there happens to be some attraction already pulling you together. Tango itself begins, then, with something as momentary and fateful as attraction, as coincidental and yet certain as chemistry. The dance itself is as much a product of that connection as the connection is of the dance.

Thomas attributes that intimacy to the fundamental sadness that lies at the heart of all tango, "one of the few Latin dances that is predominantly not happy." Its "dominant emotion is nostalgia, a sense of loss," of a past that continually haunts the present. Most tangos are structured in sections A-B-A, which are distinguished by their key signatures, major-minor-major or minor-major-minor: happy memories enclosing, or enclosed by, a sad present. For Thomas, that sadness strengthens the connection between performers and draws the audience into their aura. "There's something that's extremely powerful about that, and about sharing one's sadness with one's dance partner," he told me. "And I think that's part of the profound emotional connection in the dance." Here he grew mildly incensed. "People always say tango is sexy, tango is sensual—I *hate* that cliché that comes from that movie with Jennifer Lopez, I don't remember what it's called." He was joking, and yet not quite. "Tango is much more than that. It's an emotional connection, an emotional intimacy. And the fact that you can have such emotional intimacy with someone you're just meeting for the first time and not even talking to, and embracing in a very close embrace, where you're touching at the chest, at the cheek, at the forehead, perhaps, and you're sharing really deep feelings that connect you to your partner and to the music, I think that's why it's such a profound emotional experience. One of the things that's often quoted is '*Tango es un pensamiento triste que se baila'**—'tango is a sad thought that is danced.'" He paused thoughtfully and then modified his translation—"'that *we* dance.'"

Thomas, a classical saxophonist by training, got into tango because it's essentially chamber music, "the chamber music of dancing." Talking to him reaffirmed for me that the distinction between the composed and the improvised in live performance is perhaps less rigid than it seems. As with tango—where you improvise not only the steps but the *way* you step, the feeling and flair and the sadness—so, too, is there is an improvisatory element to every performance of composed music, not of the notes but of the *sound*. This is especially true of ensemble performances, which require the wordless, spontaneous coordination of fingers and bows—creating a shared interpretation of each phrase, or even each note, in a given moment among all the players. I'd felt that the first time my high school quartet played "Por una Cabeza" in recital: At one point in the music, when the first articulation of the *habanera*—the most famous and recognizable tango rhythm, *ba-dum dum dum*—came rolling into the chorus, all of a sudden our sounds and articulations seemed to unite themselves, to be drawn together in a kind of magnetic resonance. I felt a sort of zooming in, a closing of the distance between us

---

* Attributed to tango composer Enrique Santos Discepolo (1901–1951).

and a deepening, as though our sounds had touched and a fire erupted between them. The notes weren't improvised, but the musicality was—the inflection and articulation of the phrase, the details of melody and countermelody and texture and rhythm were different from how we'd played it in rehearsals, yet completely simultaneous and in sync.

During our interview, I asked Thomas if he had ever experienced that kind of connection with a stranger. He had mentioned that professional tango couples rarely perform with new partners, that it takes "years of experience together" to build up "that sense of empathy, of intimacy, of connection, of synchronization, of hearing the music in similar ways, responding to each other's bodies," so that even during improvised sessions of *tango salon* they dance with complete confidence, the knowledge of each other's bodies, an intuition honed over time. I wondered if it was possible to feel that instantly: for two bodies and souls to meet and recognize each other for the first time.

Thomas nodded. "It is possible, and it's rare. From my experience I can say that it has happened." He settled back and told me the story with a sort of clipped relentless Hemingwayesque nostalgia:

"Once in Buenos Aires, three or four years ago, I was at a *milonga* in San Telmo, and it was, I don't know, three in the morning, and I went there with a friend of mine, Javier. I didn't really know anyone, but he had some friends, so we sat down, had a drink. I was watching the floor; there weren't very many people there, it was late. And there was this woman—I had seen her before; she was a DJ at another *milonga*, called Café Vinilo, in Palermo, but we had never danced. And I saw her dancing with Javier, and Javier came back to the table, and I was drinking, and I looked at her and she looked at me, and I gave her the *cabeceo* and she accepted, so we met on the floor and we danced. And it was our first *tanda*, and it was one *d'arienzo*. *D'arienzo* is very rhythmic, quite fast, with a lot of syncopation, so you really have to know the music in order to dance it rhythmically and accurately.

"And she and I connected immediately. We danced this *tanda* with, I don't know, perfection, in terms of musicality and connection, and it was the first time I'd ever danced with her. And we had an amazing *tanda*; we both loved it. And then a year went by, and I never saw her—until a year later, I went to a *milonga* again with my friend Javier, and I still remembered that night, that *tanda* in Buenos Aires. And she had forgotten who I was! I was just startled—how could you forget that *tanda* that we had, you know, that's what I was thinking. And Javier, he told me in Spanish—'Well, what did you think? We Argentinians go out dancing every night, it couldn't have been that special!' But there's a happy ending to the story. Eventually, we danced again, and it was good, and I saw her again in Europe, and again in Argentina. Now we're friends; now we dance with each other. I'll see her soon in Argentina, when I go back again. And it's all because of that amazing *tanda* that happened, that can happen even when you've never danced with someone before."

––

In his 1999 lecture entitled "The High Imagination," on improvisation, drugs, and rock and roll, the late scholar-critic and blues saxophonist David Lenson described

> an ineffable mode of consciousness that musicians call "the ESP." This is the ability to know a split second in advance what the other members of the band are going to do. Once you've acquired the ESP, it becomes almost impossible to commit a major blunder, like playing through a stop or an ending. You can hear a rhythmic punctuation coming at least a beat or two ahead, even if it happens spontaneously. The ESP also senses dynamics, as the band's volume goes up or down for dramatic effect.

Lenson, who performed with Muddy Waters, Buddy Guy, and John Lee Hooker (whom he met for the first time "in the backseat of a limousine minutes before taking the stage in front of eight thousand people"), characterizes the group ESP as the "complete internalization of a form, so that it becomes invisible." Each member of the improvising group has to inhabit that baseline of musical consciousness which constitutes knowledge of a form, a template on which to give the music shape and direction in time. From there, each musician is responsible for creating the music in time, for unspooling the phrases from the cosmic silence that lies before them. Lenson, quoting Coleridge, described improvisation as "the eternal act of creation in the infinite I AM."

This is because the temporal structures of improvised music differ from the current of time that constitutes composed, prepracticed pieces, where you always have to be thinking downstream, remembering ahead, in a sense. Instead, improvisation is like going over a waterfall again and again; there's a void opening up before every moment, and you plunge over the edge and yet somehow never fall, never reach the other side, even as you hurl yourself over again and again; and when you look back you've *created* a river, the very current you've been sailing down. Like the particles that instantaneously sync their polarities, to improvise with someone else is to pinpoint a moment of intersection in time, between past and future, you and me—to seize life and hold it still. Each moment melts like an individual snowflake and yet is replaced, simultaneously, by another which is wholly different and equally beautiful, so that you inhabit a present that is continuous and yet made up of individual moments falling and faintly falling, the drifted accumulation of the past.* To improvise is to reiterate the momentary again and again, but also to affirm its part in the completeness of things, the continuity of time.

To me, that "eternal act" is nothing less than the creation of what T. S. Eliot called a "still point" of time's turning world: neither past nor future, "neither ascent nor decline," "neither from nor towards." To improvise one must be wholly, almost ecstatically present, and reaffirm that presentness in each moment. To improvise with other people, then, is to share that ecstasy with them. The togetherness enabled by Lenson's "ESP" derives from a shared sense of time, yet one that is far from mechanical; indeed, you are so deeply in sync that you can be completely *un*mechanical and still stay together. Each person contributes how they hear and want to hear the music, and the group absorbs all of those interpretations. In tango, Thomas says, the true freedom of improvisation is "not about anticipating what's coming next; it's understanding the music so well that at any moment, wherever you happen to be in the dance—in a pause, in

---

* The physicist Carlo Rovelli in his book *The Order of Time*: "[Time] is like holding a snowflake in your hands: gradually, as you study it, it melts between your fingers and vanishes" (p. 3).

a turn, in a walk—you can express really fine details of melody and countermelody, of rhythm, of the violin and the piano and the bandoneon, and you can bring out texture. And your partner can even surprise you—by hearing things that you hear, but bringing them out even more. And this is the kind of partner I love to have, when their musicality is so profound that it changes the way you hear the music, and it changes the way you experience the music." To improvise with others, then, is to experience something more than the infinite subjectivity of time: It is to know that those individual subjectivities can be unified. In order to move with your partner perfectly in time, you have to know you are both *feeling* time in the same way. In short, it's entanglement: the certainty of simultaneity, the eternal act of creation in the infinite *we are.*

—

Over the next four Mondays, I went back to the Quad to keep practicing tango. The class learned that "every step in tango can be described in terms of accelerations and pauses," and practiced leading and following with our eyes closed. We learned *la entrada*, where for a moment the man extends his leg toward the woman's, so that briefly, just barely, his foot grazes the inside of her ankle. ("Go with confidence and retreat with confidence," Thomas said. "It's like touching fire.") As the weeks progressed and everyone got more comfortable and automatic with the steps, people began to develop distinct styles. Sometimes I wouldn't dance but would sit back and watch the others to get a sense of how they moved: Barbara, a clarinetist who danced with both an ease and a humility; Shihan, whose movements were as delicate as the gold high-heeled sandals she wore to each lesson. There was one guy, Anton, who always wore green linen trousers and a black turtleneck and was really good; he had the tension-release, accelerate-and-pause thing down. Another lady in a blue blouse, whose name in all those weeks I never caught, danced with her eyes closed.

I never got over my shyness completely, but I did love going to tango class on those Mondays. I loved the metaphors in Thomas's and Silvana's descriptions of the dance, how such a physical thing could (and perhaps had to be) made metaphorical; it reminded me of my violin teacher in my first years of college, Ying, for whom finding the right sound was as much about feeling "the ball of energy in your core" and the "taut pearl-string of your spine" as about where you placed the bow on the strings and how fast you vibrated the fingers of your left hand. Above all, I loved to watch week after week these different people entering—and to join them in entering—the aura of sweat and heat and pheromone and breath that emanates uniquely from every human being, that halo of human energy in such an earthly space. Perhaps this, too, is the sadness of tango: the proximity of beating hearts ticking out their own private time. It reminded me of how once when I was little, watching a movie with my dad, I laid my head on his chest only to be terrified by the soft thudding of his heart, how its very continuity seemed a kind of countdown toward something finite and inevitable.

During the last class before the *milonga*, Thomas and Silvana had us try dancing "La Cumparsita" (from *comparsa*, "carnival"), a brisk style of tango from the 1920s that is played at the end of most *milongas*. "La Cumparsita" is known for its urgent tempo and propulsive syncopations, but there are also splendid moments of intense and high suspension when, suddenly, the rhythm played by the castanets and piano drops out and the violin is left soaring perilously, alone, until the piano rolls back gutturally into time and the castanets begin snapping out the beat once more. Thomas was teaching us how to incorporate pauses in our dancing when the rhythm stops—how to hold your body for that moment of stillness, how to intuit when the pauses would occur and to feel how long that split second would last—in other words, how to feel the push and pull of time.

I was dancing with Ana, who had graciously allowed me to be her partner again. (She was often late to class because she was coming from her lab; until she arrived, there would be an odd number of us, and since I wasn't technically enrolled I would hang back and wait to dance. Thus she often got saddled with me.) I should say now that in spite of Thomas's and Silvana's best efforts, when it came to dancing tango I was an absolute travesty. I could never tell which way I was supposed to turn, which, unfortunately, was a problem, since turns constitute about 50 percent of the dance. This particular evening, I kept turning the opposite way and continuing through the pauses, so that I consistently ended up with the wrong leg awkwardly extended over Ana's. Ana was very nice about it.

"Come, come, I'll show you," said Silvana, sweeping in suddenly to be my salvation (or, more likely, to save Ana from me). "Like this," she said, grabbing me by the hand and around the waist. She started to turn, spinning us across the dance floor. There was an urgency and a grace to the way she moved, a quickness that made me move with her automatically. "Don't think," she said, *dance.*" "Um," I replied. But there was something about her energy, her urgency which was at once invitation and command, that allowed my body to move in time with hers. My feet took the right steps of their own accord; I turned in the right direction; I knew where she was going before she went there. Even the pauses seemed predestined and yet of a moment's whim—I knew, through her, when the beat was going to stop for a second and then start again, though I couldn't have told you how. The whole thing lasted about ten seconds, until I started to think again and promptly stepped on her foot.

I stood there for a moment, astonished: for the first time in my life, I had danced. Not the blind, beer-fueled collective jumping of college dorm parties or the awkward swaying that prevails among single people during the slow dances at cousins' weddings, but *real* dancing, with one other person, with a partner who made me move and moved with me. I hadn't known what I was doing, and yet I *had*: feeling the energy of her torso, the lightness of her arms, the sureness of her feet from impulse to impulse, that miraculous synergy which requires both a certainty and a forgetting when, enlivened by that spontaneous connection to another human being, the body takes over the mind.

Two weeks before the final *milonga*, Thomas asked if I would be willing to play some tango violin at the event, as an interlude between *tandas*. He knew a really good pianist, come to think of it, who might be able to play with me, one of his thesis advisees in the Comp Lit department. Did I happen to know Mateo Lincoln, by chance?

Coincidentally, I did. Not particularly well— we'd met our freshman year, after being put in touch by his second cousin whom I vaguely knew from Denver, but we had never really spoken, much less played together. When we met again, I knew we would be friends. Mateo is one of those rare people with the uncanny ability to anticipate your feelings or needs before you know them yourself. Once, when we were messaging back and forth about setting up rehearsals, he apologized for the recent and sudden dearth of exclamation points in his messages; for some reason, the exclamation-point key on his computer had stopped working, and since he was normally "a serial exclamation-point user," he didn't want me to think he was mad or annoyed. He is a composer and a pianist and is often running somewhere because he is volunteering his time; he is writing music for a friend's short film as a favor, or stepping in at the last minute as an organist and music director for a church service. In the week leading up to the performance, for several days he gave his time to me.

We were going to play "Invierno Porteño," or "Winter," the last movement of Astor Piazzolla's *Four Seasons of Buenos Aires*. (The allusion is to Vivaldi's famous *Four Seasons*; Piazzolla, who helped incorporate tango into the classical canon, took snatches of Vivaldi's themes and inverted and transposed and otherwise renovated them—the seasons in the southern hemisphere are reversed, after all.) I loved playing with Mateo. Our styles clicked, and "Invierno Porteño" came together easily. But a few days before the performance, Thomas asked if we could add one of his favorite tangos: "Cafe 1930," the second movement of Piazzolla's *Histoire du Tango* (which is a survey of tango's evolution through the twentieth century, beginning in the bordellos of

Buenos Aires and ending with an avant-garde *concert d'aujourd'hui*). "Oh, the *milonga* is going to be so low-key," he said when I told him that another piece, um, might be a little tricky to put together, since there wasn't much time left to rehearse. "You can just wing it, right? Look, don't worry about it—it's such a good piece, you *have* to play it!"

The day of the performance, Mateo and I spent almost five hours locked up in a practice room, trying frantically to learn "Cafe 1930." It's one of those pieces that's not hard until, well, it *is*—the slow opening melody lulls you into the purple haze of nostalgia, until a surge of sudden feeling culminates in a burst of rapid sixteenth notes that are very, very hard to play in tune. I believe we only got through the piece once without having to stop before it was time to go onstage. We still weren't at the point where we knew with confidence what notes would come next. In an unimprovised performance, which is what this was supposed to be, anticipation requires memory, and memory enables anticipation: You rely on your knowledge of what comes next in order to think and listen ahead. I could barely remember the music's main theme, much less the secondary melodies and thematic deconstructions that followed. At least we'd have the sheet music, but notes alone do not a performance make; we'd have to rely on our intuition for the more important parts, the musicality and the coordination. Every moment would essentially be a revelation, to put it mildly, and that's generally *not* what you want in front of an audience. I couldn't decide whether I needed to throw up or pass out, but at that point there wasn't time for either.

Just before we went onstage to play the music we didn't really know how to play, I remembered something Thomas had told me during our interview. When he was younger and playing more saxophone, he suffered from crippling performance anxiety. He shied away from performing for a while because of his nerves—that is, until he took up dancing tango. He found that when he was dancing, even performing or competing, he was able to relax in a way he had rarely been able to before. He attributes that reassurance to having a partner, to the closeness and equality they shared onstage. It's different than the relationship that exists between, say, a soloist and a collaborative pianist, or even members of an orchestra; indeed, it is only to be found in chamber music, where all the parts are equal in their importance and their vulnerability. As a player, being with others gives you something to focus on instead of how nervous you feel. "The thing you *can* do is be with them; to say, whatever happens, I have you, you have me," Thomas said. He remembers thinking, *"This* is my way back into music—through tango."

I looked at Mateo. "Whatever happens," he said, smiling, and I smiled back, and we went onstage to perform.

The *milonga* was being held at Holden Chapel, a small chapel in the college's central yard. Thomas had cleared away the rows of chairs and turned the lights down low, transfiguring the chapel's nave into an elegant (if makeshift) dance floor and stage. We were going to play between two *tandas* about halfway through, and before our set we got to watch a bit from the wings. A lot of people from the class had turned up, but there were also some I'd never seen before, a few middle-aged husbands and wives who danced mostly with other people and one young couple who danced almost exclusively with each other. Many of the new people danced flawlessly; it looked a lot like date night for a bunch of very experienced amateurs. But I also saw, with happiness, how well my classmates were dancing, improvising with ease not only with one another but with people they had never met.

"Invierno Porteño" went fine, just as Mateo and I had prepared it; the notes and phrasing were all there, though we could have made more of the timing, dared to push and pull the phrases with a little more fun and spontaneity. That was largely my fault: I wasn't thinking much about what was happening now, so focused was I on what was coming and how I probably wouldn't be able to play it. But Mateo smiled encouragingly at me just before we began "Cafe 1930." *Just wing it*, I thought as the applause from the first piece died down, *he's with you*.

Mateo played the first bars, a slow, breathing

succession of chords, rolling them delicately as though on a mandolin. They were so beautiful that I was taken out of my thoughts and instead began hearing, in my head, how the violin part would sound in counterpoint to his playing. When someone plays with that kind of deep feeling, it's almost impossible *not* to play toward that person, *not* to send your sound out so that it rises to meet theirs. I stopped trying to remember the notes or to think ahead, and instead focused just on creating, in order to join Mateo in the purple world that had begun to exist with his first notes. Nothing, it seemed, could disturb its smooth melancholy revolutions, not with both of us held in the gravity of that mind-set. We'd get to tricky cadences where it was difficult to align the violin part with the piano, places where we'd had a lot of trouble in rehearsal, and I would brace myself and listen for Mateo and at the same time just play it the way I felt, hoping to God he and I would stay together. And we *would*. At those moments it seemed as though we'd passed through a filter and some inner polarization had snapped into place, and we'd emerged on the other side of that instant with a wide-eyed clarity that kept us going. I began to feel that I knew, before each note, how it was meant to be played at that particular moment, in that particular performance by Mateo and me. We were bound to each other, yet I felt in that very binding a kind of freedom, because I could do whatever I wanted and knew he would be with me, and that whatever he did, I, too, would be with him. That freedom astonished me and made me shudder. It seemed that inside the very music we were dancing, two leaping particles in a world of our own. Or, perhaps, that our entanglement *was* the music, the sound waves the reverberation of our synchronized fields of energy. As "Cafe 1930" unfurled itself in time, I felt the way I had when I'd danced with Silvana: that we didn't need to know what would come next because it didn't matter, whatever happened would be right; that we were free, creating time; indeed, that we didn't exist in time, but, rather, time lived in us.

I wonder what that means, exactly: for time to live *in us*. It's a feeling I have whenever I am playing well—not just getting the notes but *really* playing just the way I want, or sometimes even when I am simply listening to music—one I cannot shake. It's a strange feeling, beautiful but also eerie: not only that you can step into time's flow, but that you *are* the flow itself. I suppose at the heart of that feeling, too, lies the real trouble with time: the terrifying prospect that if time is so subjective, then we are necessarily alone in our unique experience of it. But isn't it *because* time lives in us that we can shape it, sculpt it into phrases and cadences and *giros* and *ochos*; still it if not stop it, bend it if not vanquish it. And share it. For me, it is the presence of another person— Mateo when we performed "Cafe 1930," Silvana for those ten eternal seconds when we danced, a face

in the crowd in a dimly lit concert room—that has
the power to take me out of my self-consciousness
of my own time, in a rare improvisatory moment
unencumbered by any thought of past or future, a
leaping wide across the universe. In that moment
of high and unified suspension, with you and I
poised at the top of the parabola—neither ascent
nor decline, neither from nor towards—here life
stands still, because I am freed, by your presence,
from myself. The heart stirs: The particles sync,
the dancers move; and that movement itself is stillness. As for the dance itself, our brief timelessness,
I cannot say how long it will last, cannot place it in
time—because it is within the stillness of our close
embrace that time, at last, ceases to matter.

Coda

Memory Is a Hologram

A few months ago it struck me, while I was writing this book, that I can probably no longer call myself a violinist in the traditional sense of the word. I had gone about twenty days or so without so much as tuning my instrument, not out of despair or spite, but because I was busy writing. And, strangely enough, I hadn't really missed it. At the same time, I was listening to and feeling and understanding music more deeply and clearly than I ever had. Writing about the pieces of my childhood, the pieces I still love best, gave me a sense of grateful belonging to them that I had sought all my life and had never quite achieved in practice. I know what the Chaconne is *about*, at least as I interpret it, now that I have written about the experience of learning and relearning it; I can tell you just how "La Campanella" or those double octaves in Sibelius ought to be executed, from this distance in time. In short, I feel like a better violinist than I ever have been—I guess as long as I'm not playing.

It's not a perfect solution, of course. I still feel guilty; I still miss the part of my life that cradled, and was cradled by, the violin. But for me, writing is a way of continuing to be a musician, and of growing as a musician, because without music I don't think I would have anything to write about, or at least anything worthwhile to say. And writing about time in music, in particular, opened up to me a world of scientific research that I had never known: In order to write credibly, I had to dig into the physics metaphors and biological responses that connect musical temporality to something larger and more fundamental about the human experience. Time, or at least our perception of its passage, is too complicated a subject to examine from either a humanistic or a scientific angle alone. Each needs the other, points inevitably toward the other.

That same desire for comprehensiveness and unity lies at the heart of physics itself, which is one reason why I love to read about it, love to study it, limited though my technical knowledge may be. Physicists have long sought a "theory of everything," what Stephen Hawking and Leonard Mlodinow, in a 2010 article in *Scientific American*, called "one complete and consistent set of fundamental laws of nature that explain every aspect of reality." At the moment, two main theoretical frameworks, taken together, provide the closest thing we have to a theory of everything (or TOE, as it is abbreviated by scientists). One applies to the realm of the cosmically large: general relativity, Einstein's theory that matter and energy bend space-time gravitationally.

The other governs the world of the infinitesimally small: quantum mechanics, whose Standard Model deals with three nongravitational forces, indeed leaving gravity out of the equation entirely.

These two frameworks function well for describing our world, since it is almost always clear in which contexts to apply one and not the other. Almost always, that is, except for in places where the cosmic runs up against the infinitesimal, such as black holes, where "lots of mass and energy twist space so tightly that even electrons and their ilk can't help but take notice," writes the physics journalist Charlie Wood. Gravity can curve space-time so strongly that it produces a singularity, a point where an enormous amount of mass is condensed into such an infinitely tiny space that a black hole or a Big Bang results. The singularity itself is so small that the effects of quantum mechanics become impossible to ignore, pointing toward some inevitable, undiscovered connection between the gravity that produced it and the quantum theory that helps govern it. And so somehow our intuition remains that there must be something more, something higher, out there for us to discover; we are left still with our human longing to arrive at the oneness of space, time, and experience across the universe.

One way of bridging this divide—a new field, which began in the 1990s with work by theorists Gerard 't Hooft, Leonard Susskind, and Juan Maldacena—is the "holographic principle," the notion that our three-dimensional, gravitational world is essentially a holographic image encoded in tiny bits of quantum information. "According to 't Hooft," Susskind wrote in his groundbreaking 1994 paper "The World as a Hologram," "the combination of quantum mechanics and gravity requires the three-dimensional world to be an image of data that can be stored on a two-dimensional projection much like a holographic image." In other words, gravity and nongravitational quantum forces—at odds with one another under general relativity and the Standard Model—are inextricably coupled in a universe of two dimensions that is somehow "rich enough to describe all three-dimensional phenomena." Maldacena, advancing Susskind and 't Hooft's work, quantitatively constructed a toy holographic universe—a theoretical "universe in a bottle"— whose interior bulk of gravity-producing space-time "maps to a network of quantum particles living on the bottle's rigid, gravity-free surface," as the science journalist Natalie Wolchover writes. If we are to imagine Maldacena's theoretical bottle as a real one, what looks to us like the bottle's contents—its cosmic Coca-Cola, let's say—exists simultaneously as a volume of liquid and as an image of those contents only, a projection on the bottle's exterior. And here's the real magic: The dynamical gravity of the liquid sloshing inside the bottle emerges entirely *from* the quantum mechanics of the image on its surface, the hologram stretched along the contoured boundary of the glass.

The question remains, of course, whether the mathematics of a bottled universe can describe the operations of one like ours, whose only boundary is "the infinite future." But if the theory is right, there are devastating implications for the divergence between our sense of reality and reality itself. The three-dimensionality of space that we perceive may merely be an illusion of depth and reality. Our perception essentially squeezes the universe into a ball, rolls it toward the overwhelming question of whether we are, or are not, as we appear to be on the surface of things.

And yet it's not such a strange idea, perhaps, when you consider that our world is full of holograms. Music, for instance, is holographic: A written score contains all the myriad possibilities of a full performance, so many of which are themselves unwritten; the way we are to experience its sounds in time is condensed into a pictorial procession of notes along the staves, the tiny fs for forte and dots representing staccato and hairpin markings for crescendos that bind a piece's universe in a hieroglyphic nutshell of represented sound. Writing, too, in that sense, and the equations that describe our physical world are also holograms—as is DNA, which encodes all biology in permutations of the letters A, C, G, and T. Indeed, every language, every form of communication or expression, is a way of describing the high-dimensional information of experience via black marks on a page, a condensation of our lived experience of time into that which we can write, record, remember, relive.

I suppose this is my justification for why I've written this book the way I have, yoking together disparate topics that, on the surface, don't seem to have much to do with one another. The discussions of music and science are holograms of a kind, encodings of experience and information that offer different projections for how to understand time from inside one world, which, in turn, might shed light on how time passes in another. For me personally, the book is meant to be a hologram of sorts, too: for all my memories of this thing I loved, that I will both always have and can never have again.

In their *Scientific American* article, Hawking and Mlodinow wrote that there is no ultimate way of knowing whether reality is what we perceive it to be, in part because "according to quantum physics, the past, like the future, is indefinite and exists only as a spectrum of possibilities. Even the universe as a whole has no single past or history." I have written about my past in order to understand it for myself, and in doing so have necessarily *re*written it, altering not the facts themselves but the way they converge to make narrative, to create meaning. I feel less, now, that I lost or gave up the chance to become a musician; rather that my being a musician was a necessary and wonderful thing, for the time that I was, and that eventually that time had to come to an end. Somehow looking back on and recording the choice has altered that choice, or at least its consequence. This is what I have to tell myself in order to live with the facts as they are—and yet it really does seem that way to me, that this is the only possible ending for the story. This is also what makes writing frightening, at least to my mind: the fact that it can change the past so effortlessly, and solidify that change into reality. And yet I tell myself, too, that part of the marvel of living must surely be in our struggle to understand our lives both as we narrate them through memory and as they really are; and that in doing so we might perhaps get closer to knowing the beginning and the end of time.

Acknowledgments

This section is the hardest to write of all. My heart is so full. I am grateful to so many who helped and encouraged and inspired me along the way, particularly the following people.

Erika Goldman, to whom I am grateful for taking a chance on my manuscript and am very much indebted to for so steadfastly walking this path with me; she helped me envision what this book could be and contributed so many detailed, incisive, and imaginative ideas on how to expand what originated as my college thesis. Her big heart dared me to open myself up to possibilities I hadn't considered before, and her team at Bellevue Literary Press—Laura Hart, Molly Mikolowski, and Joe Gannon—brought my manuscript to life. Thank you also to Drs. Anirrudh Patel, Thomas Wisniewski, Charles Limb, and Robin Carhart-Harris for giving so generously of their time and expertise as I researched, wrote, and rewrote; Field Brown, whose anecdote about stammering and time in "Untrainment" unlocked much of that chapter for me; Silvana Brizuela, again Thomas Wisniewski, and the entire 7:00 P.M. class of the 2018–2019 Harvard Argentine Tango Society for being so warm and welcoming and letting a noob like me join in; and Mateo Lincoln for being such a willing and wonderful tango partner and an even better friend. I am also indebted to Professors Marc Shell and Darcy Frey, who have endlessly encouraged and supported me both during college and now, as I attempt to navigate the strangeness of life after. Thank you so much to Michael Allen and Christopher Spaide for helping me think critically about time and the music of poetry, and to Professor Helen Vendler for the two joyful semesters I got to spend as your student and for taking me to my first talk at the Radcliffe Institute. Christina Thompson offered insightful edits on "Untrainment," and I am grateful to her and the entire staff of the *Harvard Review* for first publishing that piece; thank you also to Professor Richard Hoffman for your kindness and encouragement, and the staff of *Solstice Literary Magazine* for taking on "The Still Point of the Turning World." My classmates in Professor Hoffman's nonfiction workshop at Emerson College offered me so much discerning feedback and empathetic support; thank you to each one of you. And I am grateful to Julia DeBenedictis for her generous editorial eye and the gift of her brilliant, loving, once-in-a-lifetime friendship. How fortunate I am to be on this journey with you, to the villa and beyond.

It has been my privilege to learn from so many musicians, classical and otherwise, who have filled my life with beauty. I am particularly grateful to Basil and Jennifer Vendryes for the abiding love (and numerous lessons, chamber coachings, and delicious meals) they have shared with our family over the years, and for the magical summer I got to spend as Basil's student in Acqui Terme, Italy, relearning the Chaconne. Claude Sim and Donald Weilerstein opened my mind to new ways of thinking about the mind-body connection and how it relates to violin playing, and patiently helped me work toward freeing my music from the constraints of an adolescent technique. And to Jake Leventhal, Zach Heckendorf, Ju-Hyun Lee, Aristo Sham, and all the members of Music 189 and InTune String Ensemble; some of the happiest times of my life have been when we played together. I also owe a great debt to the entire staff of the Harvard Music Department, in particular Kaye Denny and Charles Stillman, who gave me a home at Harvard, and Jessica Bodner, Daniel Chong, Ken Hamao, and Kee Kim of the Parker Quartet, who have looked out for me, taken care of me, and encouraged both my playing and my love of chamber music. Most of all, I am grateful to Ying Xue and James and Jackie Maurer, for everything you have taught me, and for giving me the courage to keep going.

Finally, three most special thank-yous:

To my adviser and mentor, Michael Pollan. Thank you for every link you sent, every insight you shared, every encouraging email. As hard as the subject matter was at times, your thoughtful and often humorous critiques made writing this book a joy. Working with you has changed my mind about what's possible for me with both writing and music, and getting to be your student has changed my life. In your pursuit of the truth, you behold beauty and illuminate it for others. I will be forever admiring and grateful.

To Nisarga Paul, who reassured me with his close, patient, and insightful editing of the manuscript's scientific elements, and to whom the connection between the path integral and improvisation belongs, for your brilliant help and knowledge, your steadfast support, and for expanding and enriching my appreciation of physics and its poetry.

To Emo, Uncle, Gabriel, and Sebastian, Harabuji and Halmoni and Grampa, for watching over and taking care of our family, and for reminding me to find grace in all things; and to Aunt Mary, Uncle Dave, Dr. Sun Halmoni, and all the Rohs and Chois, who when we lost one side of our family adopted us and shared with us more love than we knew our hearts could hold. To Eloise, Eliot, and Aidan: I love you, and am beyond grateful that we can still laugh together and keep one another in line. I learn so much from each of you about how to live meaningfully and with purpose and joy. And, most of all, to Uhmma—for reminding me to notice something beautiful every day; for all our conversations and your close and insightful editing of every draft; for keeping all of us together no matter what turn our travels take; for giving us music; for loving us so well. When I am with you, time stands still.

Credits

Notes

PRELUDE

Page 14: **"A future event causes the atom to decide its past"**: Morgan, "Scientists Show Future Events Decide What Happens in the Past."

Page 16: **"the mystery of time is ultimately, perhaps, more about ourselves than about the cosmos"**: Rovelli, *The Order of Time*, 5.

UNTRAINMENT

Page 18: **4/4 time**: The most common of all time signatures (literally referred to as "common time"), where the quarter note gets the beat and there are four beats to a bar.

Page 21: **a form "in which the leading theme recurs between sections and then returns to complete the composition"**: "Rondo," *Oxford English Dictionary*.

Page 24: **Rhythm is at the heart of that arrangement, on every scale**: "[R]hythm is often considered the most basic aspect of music, and is increasingly thought to be a fundamental organizing principle of brain function." Patel and Iversen, "The Evolutionary Neuroscience of Musical Beat Perception."

Page 24: **"measured flow"**: "Rhythm," *Oxford English Dictionary*.

186

Page 28: **"a perceived periodic pulse that listeners use to guide their movements and performers use to coordinate their actions"**: Patel and Iversen, "The Evolutionary Neuroscience of Musical Beat Perception."

Page 28: **"a task which is trivially easy for humans, even for those with no musical training"**: Ibid.

Pages 31-32: **"focal reductions in activity" in the brain's motor-control regions when subjects were asked to perform even trivial fine-motor tasks in front of an audience**: Yoshie et. al, "Why I Tense Up When You Watch Me."

Page 32: **According to Patel, yes, it's possible**: However, studies specifically on performance anxiety and entrainment would need to be conducted in order to prove this connection conclusively.

Page 32: **"Specifically, ASAP predicts that the disruption of normal activity in motor planning regions will impair beat perception"**: Patel and Iversen, "The Evolutionary Neuroscience of Musical Beat Perception."

Page 32: **"persistent low-level muscle tension in the arm and shoulder, induced by the presence of an audience, [led] to increased keystroke force resulting in a loss of fine control of dynamics and temporal fluency within musical performances"**: Yoshie et al., "Why I Tense Up When You Watch Me," in reference to her 2009 paper in *Experimental Brain Research*, entitled "Music Performance Anxiety in Skilled Pianists."

Pages 39–40: **A 2015 study of "statistical universals"**
of human music, led by musicologist Patrick
Savage and published in the *Proceedings of*
the National Academy of Sciences: Savage et al.,
"Statistical universals reveal the structures and
function of human music."

Page 40: **"auditory cheesecake"**: Steven Pinker's
explanation, in his 1997 book, *How the Mind Works,*
of music as "an exquisite confection crafted to
tickle the sensitive spots of at least six of our mental
faculties,"—useful for stimulating "the pleasure
circuits of the brain . . . without the inconvenience of
wringing bona fide fitness increments from the harsh
world." Pinker, *How the Mind Works,* 534, 524.

A SIXTH SENSE: NOTES ON IMPROVISATION

Page 53: **"composition is just improvisation slowed**
down." Quoted in Michelle Mercer's 2007 book
Footprints: The Life and Music of Wayne Shorter,
140.

Page 53: **"[there is] scarcely a musical technique or**
form of composition that did not originate in
improvisatory performance or was not essentially
influenced by it": Ferand, *Improvisation in Nine*
Centuries of Western Music, 5.

Page 54: **"perhaps the West's signal musical**
distinction": Taruskin, *The Oxford History of Western*
Music, xxiii.

Page 55: **"with all necessary ornamentation written**
out in an appropriate manner for those who
might otherwise be unable to interpret the
score improvisationally": Moore, "The Decline of
Improvisation in Western Art Music," 72.

Page 55: **caused "aspiring art musicians [to become] increasingly self-conscious in the performance of canonized works, and [they] tended to rely more heavily on the interpretative advice of influential music professionals, rather than untutored instinct"**: Ibid., 73.

Page 56: **"the creation of a musical work, or the final form of a musical work, as it is being performed . . . and to some extent every improvisation rests on a series of conventions or implicit rules"**: Bruno Nettl quoted in Wright, "Investigating Improvisation," 7.

Page 57: **"It is only an effective means of expression when incorporating a vocabulary, whether cognitively or intuitively understood, common to a group of individuals"**: Moore, "The Decline of Improvisation in Western Art Music," 64.

Page 60: **"improvisation forms part of their core musical behavior"**: Barrett et. al, "Classical creativity: A functional magnetic resonance imaging (fMRI) investigation of pianist and improviser Gabriela Montero," 4.

Page 61: **"turning on a faucet"**: Ibid., 10.

Page 65: **"remote and pushed into the background, as if in most secret caverns"**: Augustine, *Confessions*, 10.17. 188–89.

Page 65: **"by thinking we, as it were, gather together ideas which the memory contains in a dispersed and disordered way, and by concentrating our attention we arrange them in order as if ready to hand, stored in the very memory where previously they lay hidden, scattered, and neglected"**: Ibid., 10.18. 189.

Page 65: **"the mind knows things it does not know it knows"**: Ibid., 185 n. 12.

Page 67: **the *actual* path that the particle traverses**: Feynman, "The Principle of Least Action."

Page 76: **"artists like GM also call on their emotions and personal identity when performing"—even if these emotions are not "the primary subject of conscious thought"**: Barrett et. al, "Classical creativity," 11.

SYMMETRY BREAKING

Page 91: **"Chua is prescribing life motivated by perfectionism—fear of failure, fear of disappointment"; a "vicious form of unhappiness"**: Carter, "Chinese Mothers Controversy."

Page 91: **"[q]uit the piano and the violin"**: Waldman, "In Defense of the Guilty, Ambivalent, Preoccupied Western Mom."

Page 93: **anywhere between 15 and 40 percent of the undergraduate populations at the top conservatories in the United States**: data collected from DATA USA, College Tuition Compare, Univstats, and College Simply.

Page 93: **according to a 2016 diversity report conducted by the League of American Orchestras, approximately 9 percent of professional orchestral musicians identify as Asian or Pacific Islander**: "Racial/Ethnic and Gender Diversity in the Orchestra Field," 3.

Page 93: "[s]uch an exaggerated perception of Asian dominance in classical music suggests that Asian musicians are racially marked": Yoshihara, *Musicians from a Different Shore*, 4–5.

Page 93–94: "model minority: those who rise in the existing social structure through hard work and attain success in Western culture without posing a direct challenge to the economic and political status quo": Ibid., 3–4.

CHACONNE

Page 115: no evidence that Bach wrote the Chaconne as a memorial to her: In a 2013 essay for the *Los Angeles Review of Books*, music historian Michael Markham traces the myth back to a 1994 article by "German musicologist Helga Thoene . . . [who] sought to prove the connection [between the Chaconne and Maria Barbara's death] by locating hidden melodies scattered about the texture of the score, all of which reference mourning or death-related chorale tunes. . . . The themes she found, however, were nothing more than rising or falling scale fragments."

Page 115: "Here's the story, please do what you can to make violinists aware, as playing the Chaconne without the backstory is like trying to appreciate the Mona Lisa by touching it with your eyes closed": Answer posted by Trevor Ford in the online forum Quora, part of the thread entitled, "Is there an underlying symbolic meaning in Bach's D minor Chaconne (violin partita no. 2), if so what?"

Page 115: **a dance in three-beat time**: According to *The Harvard Dictionary of Music* (2nd ed., 1969, p. 142), edited by Willi Apel, "[t]here is reason to believe the chaconne originally was a wild and sensual Mexican dance that was imported into Spain during the 16th century."

Page 116: **"the greatest structure for solo violin that exists"**: Yehudi Menuhin quoted in "Bach's Chaconne: Quotes," compiled by Humboldt State University Department of Music.

Page 116–117: **"not just one of the greatest pieces of music ever written, but one of the greatest achievements of any man in history. It's a spiritually powerful piece—emotionally powerful, structurally perfect"**: Joshua Bell quoted in ibid.

Page 117: **"[o]n one stave, for a small instrument, the man writes a whole world of the deepest thoughts and most powerful feelings"**: Johannes Brahms quoted in Hegelson, "The Story Behind Bach's Monumental Chaconne."

The Still Point of the Turning World

Page 143: **Carlos Gardel's "Por una Cabeza"**: Gardel (1917–1935) is one of the most celebrated singers and composers of Argentine tango of all time, and "Por una Cabeza" is perhaps his best-known tango.

Page 149: **any given particle "is entangled with many particles far outside our horizon"**: Buniy and Hsu, "Everything Is Entangled," 233–36.

Page 149: **a team at MIT demonstrated that entanglement holds true across space-time, between particles that are billions of light-years apart**: Chu, "Light from Ancient Quasars Helps Confirm Quantum Entanglement."

Page 151: **the jury is still out on whether entanglement can be extrapolated from the quantum physical to the human and biological**: "Studies of the European robin suggest that it has an internal chemical compass that utilises an astonishing quantum concept called entanglement . . . The current best guess is that this takes place inside a protein in the bird's eye, where quantum entanglement makes a pair of electrons highly sensitive to the angle of orientation of the Earth's magnetic field, allowing the bird to 'see' which way it needs to fly." Al-Khalili and McFadden, "You're Powered by Quantum Mechanics. No, Really . . ."

Page 152: **the Covenant Between the Parts in Genesis**: "And he took him all these, and divided them in the midst, and laid each half over against the other . . . And it came to pass, that, when the sun was going down, a deep sleep fell upon Abram; and, lo, a dread, even a great darkness, fell upon him . . . And it came to pass, that, when the sun went down, and there was thick darkness, behold, a smoking furnace, and a burning lamp that passed between these pieces" (Gen. 15: 10, 17). Metaphor posited by Alexander Poltorak in an article in *The Times of Israel*, referring to "when God entered into eternal covenant with Abraham (at the time called Abram)—a covenant symbolized by halved animals . . . [which] unites [God and Israel] forever into an indivisible oneness. As the Zohar says, 'Israel, Torah and God are all one.'"

Page 153: **as coincidental and yet certain as chemistry**: *Tener química* is the term used by Argentinian dancers—literally "to have chemistry."

Page 160: **"neither ascent nor decline," "neither from nor towards"**: T. S. Eliot, "Burnt Norton," II, 22, 18.

Page 166–167: **a survey of tango's evolution through the twentieth century, beginning in the bordellos of Buenos Aires and ending with an avant-garde *concert d'aujourd'hui***: The movements of *Histoire du Tango* are ordered as follows: "Bordel 1910," "Cafe 1930," "Nightclub 1960," "Concert d'aujourd'hui."

CODA: MEMORY IS A HOLOGRAM

Page 174: **"one complete and consistent set of fundamental laws of nature that explain every aspect of reality"**: Hawking and Mlodinow, "The Elusive Theory of Everything."

Page 175: **"lots of mass and energy twist space so tightly that even electrons and their ilk can't help but take notice"**: Wood, "What is Quantum Gravity?"

Page 176: **"maps to a network of quantum particles living on the bottle's rigid, gravity-free surface"**: Wolchover, "How Our Universe Could Emerge as a Hologram."

Page 177: **whose only boundary is the "infinite future"**: Ibid.

Bibliography

PRELUDE

Australian National University. "Experiment Confirms Quantum Theory Weirdness." "Science News," *ScienceDaily*, May 27, 2015. www.sciencedaily.com/releases/2015/05/150527103110.htm.

Eliot, T. S. *Collected Poems 1909–1962*. New York: Harcourt, 1963.

———. *The Confidential Clerk: A Play*. New York: Harcourt, Brace, 1954. Internet Archive. archive.org/stream/confidentialcle00elio/confidentialcle00elio_djvu.txt.

Ma, Xiao-song, et al. "Experimental Delayed-Choice Entanglement Swapping." *Nature Physics* 8, no. 6 (June 2012): 479–84. www.nature.com. doi:10.1038/nphys2294.

Manning, A. G., et al. "Wheeler's Delayed-Choice Gedanken Experiment with a Single Atom." *Nature Physics* 11, no. 7 (July 2015): 539–42. www.nature.com. doi:10.1038/nphys3343.

"Mind-Altering Quantum Experiment Shows Time Has Never Existed As We Think It Does." *Cosmic Scientist*, March 25, 2016. www.cosmicscientist.com/mind-altering-quantum-experiment-shows-time-has-never-existed-as-we-think-it-does/.

Morgan, Stephen. "Scientists Show Future Events Decide What Happens in the Past." *Digital Journal,* June 3, 2015. www.digitaljournal.com/science/experiment-shows-future-events-decide-what-happens-in-the-past/article/434829.

O'Dowd, Matt. "How the Quantum Eraser Rewrites the Past." YouTube, uploaded by PBS Space Time, August 10, 2016. www.youtube.com/watch?v=8ORLN_KwAgs.

Overbye, Dennis. "Peering Through the Gates of Time." *New York Times,* March 12, 2002. www.nytimes.com/2002/03/12/science/peering-through-the-gates-of-time.html.

Peres, Asher. "Delayed Choice for Entanglement Swapping." *Journal of Modern Optics* 47, no. 2–3, (February 2000): 139–43. arXiv.org. doi:10.1080/09500340008244032.

Rovelli, Carlo. "Perhaps Time Is the Greatest Mystery." In *The Order of Time.* New York: Riverhead Books, 2018.

Schmid, David. "Q and A: Delayed Choice Quantum Eraser—Changing the Past?" Ask the Van, Department of Physics, University of Illinois at Urbana-Champaign, January 12, 2014. van.physics.illinois.edu/qa/listing.php?id=25872.

Stevens, Wallace. "The Plain Sense of Things." In *The Collected Poems of Wallace Stevens.* New York: Knopf, 1954. www.poetryfoundation.org/poems/49420/the-plain-sense-of-things.

Thompson, Avery. "The Logic-Defying Double-Slit Experiment Is Even Weirder Than You Thought." *Popular Mechanics*, August 11, 2016. www. popularmechanics.com/science/a22280/double-slit-experiment-even-weirder/.

Walborn, Stephen P., et al. "Quantum Erasure: In Quantum Mechanics, There Are Two Sides to Every Story, but Only One Can Be Seen at a Time. Experiments Show That 'Erasing' One Allows the Other to Appear." *American Scientist* 91, no. 4 (2003): 336–343. www.jstor.org/stable/27858245.

Weizmann Institute of Science. "Quantum Theory Demonstrated: Observation Affects Reality." "Science News," *ScienceDaily*, Febuary 27, 1998. www.sciencedaily.com/releases/1998/02/980227055013.htm.

UNTRAINMENT

Carroll, Joseph. "Steven Pinker's Cheesecake for the Mind." *Philosophy and Literature* 22, no. 2, (January 1998): 478–85. *ResearchGate*. doi:10.1353/phl.1998.0036.

Darwin, Charles. *The Descent of Man and Selection in Relation to Sex*. London: Murray, 1871. www.gutenberg.org/files/2300/2300-h/2300-h.htm.

Eliot, T. S. *Collected Poems 1909–1962*. New York: Harcourt, 1963.

Miller, Geoffrey F. "Evolution of Human Music Through Sexual Selection." In *The Origins of Music*, edited by N. L. Wallin, B. Merker, and S. Brown, 329–60. Cambridge: MIT Press, 2000.

Patel, Aniruddh D. Interview with the author, October 23, 2018.

Patel, Aniruddh D., and John R. Iversen. "The Evolutionary Neuroscience of Musical Beat Perception: The Action Simulation for Auditory Prediction (ASAP) Hypothesis." *Frontiers in Systems Neuroscience* 8 (May 2014). PubMed Central. doi:10.3389/fnsys.2014.00057.

Pinker, Steven. "The Meaning of Life." In *How the Mind Works*, Norton, 1997, 521-565.

"Rhythm, n." Online Etymology Dictionary, www.oed.com.ezp-prod1.hul.harvard.edu/view/Entry/165403.

"Rondo, n." Online Etymology Dictionary, www.oed.com.ezp-prod1.hul.harvard.edu/view/Entry/167216.

Savage, Patrick E., et al. "Statistical universals reveal the structures and function of human music." *Proceedings of the National Academy of Sciences* 112, no. 29 (June 2015). doi:10.1073/pnas.1414495112.

Wang, Tianyan. "A Hypothesis on the Biological Origins and Social Evolution of Music and Dance." *Frontiers in Neuroscience* 9 (2015). doi:10.3389/fnins.2015.00030.

Yoshie, Michiko, et al. "Music Performance Anxiety in Skilled Pianists: Effects of Social-Evaluative Performance Situation on Subjective, Autonomic, and Electromyographic Reactions." *Experimental Brain Research* 199, no. 2 (November 2009): 117–26. PubMed Central. doi:10.1007/s00221-009-1979-y.

———. "Why I Tense up When You Watch Me: Inferior Parietal Cortex Mediates an Audience's Influence on Motor Performance." *Scientific Reports* 6 (January 2016): 19305. *Nature*. doi:10.1038/srep19305.

A Sixth Sense: Notes on Improvisation

"A Neurosurgeon's Overview [of] the Brain's Anatomy." American Association of Neurological Surgeons. www.aans.org/Patients/Neurosurgical-Conditions-and-Treatments/Anatomy-of-the-Brain.

"A potted history of improvisation." *National Theatre*, www.nationaltheatre.org.uk/blog/potted-history-improvisation.

Andrews-Hanna, Jessica R. "The Brain's Default Network and Its Adaptive Role in Internal Mentation." *Neuroscientist* 18, no. 3 (June 2012): 251–70. PubMed Central. doi:10.1177/1073858411403316.

"Arrow of time: New understanding of causality, free choice, and why we remember the past but not the future." *ScienceDaily*, July 28, 2015. www.sciencedaily.com/releases/2015/07/150728091946.htm.

Augustine. *Confessions*. Translated by Henry Chadwick. New York: Oxford University Press, 2009.

Barrett, Karen Chan, et al. "Classical Creativity: A Functional Magnetic Resonance Imaging (fMRI) Investigation of Pianist and Improviser Gabriela Montero." *NeuroImage* 209 (April 2020): 116496. ScienceDirect. doi:10.1016/j.neuroimage.2019.116496.

Berkowitz, Aaron L., and Daniel Ansari. "Expertise-Related Deactivation of the Right Temporoparietal Junction During Musical Improvisation." *NeuroImage* 49, no. 1 (January 2010): 712–19. ScienceDirect. doi:10.1016/j.neuroimage.2009.08.042.

Bubic, Andreja, et al. "Prediction, Cognition and the Brain." *Frontiers in Human Neuroscience* 4 (March 2010): 1–15. PubMed Central. doi:10.3389/fnhum.2010.00025.

Carhart-Harris, Robin Lester, et al. "The Entropic Brain: A Theory of Conscious States Informed by Neuroimaging Research with Psychedelic Drugs." *Frontiers in Human Neuroscience* 8 (2014): 1–22. doi:10.3389/fnhum.2014.00020.

Cheever, Thomas, et al. "NIH/Kennedy Center Workshop on Music and the Brain: Finding Harmony." *Neuron* 97, no. 6 (March 2018): 1214–18. PubMed Central. doi:10.1016/j.neuron.2018.02.004.

Dolan, David, et al. "The Improvisational State of Mind: A Multidisciplinary Study of an Improvisatory Approach to Classical Music Repertoire Performance." *Frontiers in Psychology* 9 (2018): 1341. doi:10.3389/fpsyg.2018.01341.

"Don't Do Your Best I Keith Johnstone I TEDxYYC." YouTube, uploaded by TEDx Talks, September 12, 2016. www.youtube.com/watch?v=bz9mo4qW9bc.

Dronkers, N., and J. Ogar. "Brain Areas Involved in Speech Production." *Brain* 127, no. 7 (July 2004): 1461–62. doi:10.1093/brain/awh233.

Duchen, Jessica. "Gabriela Montero—You don't hear 80 per cent of what goes on in my country." *Independent*, October 22, 2010. www.independent.co.uk/arts-entertainment/classical/features/gabriela-montero-you-dont-hear-80-per-cent-of-what-goes-on-in-my-country-2113051.html.

Feynman, Richard. "The Priciple of Least Action." In *The Feynman Lectures on Physics: New Millennium Edition*, vol. 2, edited by Michael A. Gottlieb and Rudolf Pfeiffer. New York: Basic Books, 2011, ch. 19. www.feynmanlectures.caltech.edu/II_19.html.

Gołosz, Jerzy. "Weak Interactions: Asymmetry of Time or Asymmetry in Time?" *Journal for General Philosophy of Science* 48, no. 1 (March 2017): 19–33. SpringerLink. doi:10.1007/s10838-016-9342-z.

Gopnik, Alison. "For Innovation, Dodge the Prefrontal Police." *Wall Street Journal*, April 6, 2013. www.wsj.com/articles/SB10001424127887324020504578398820516033706.

Green, Franziska. "In the 'Creative' Zone: An Interview with Dr. Charles Limb." *Brain World*, August 22, 2019. www.brainworldmagazine.com/creative-zone-interview-dr-charles-limb/.

Harte, Erin. "How Your Brain Processes Language." *Brain World*, August 18, 2020. www.brainworldmagazine.com/how-your-brain-processes-language/.

Hawking, Stephen. "The Arrow of Time." In *The Illustrated Brief History of Time*, 2nd ed, Bantam Books, 1996, 182–195.

Hermann, Steffen, and Maria Stodtmeier. "Gabriela Montero – Improvisations, Brahms & Ginastera (Full Performance)." YouTube, uploaded by Nene, June 13, 2017. www.youtube.com/watch?v=fkXG-2LukrE.

"How can Feynman's path integral formulation of quantum mechanics be explained in layman terms?" www.quora.com/How-can-Feynmans-path-integral-*Quora*, formulation-of-quantum-mechanics-be-explained-in-layman-terms.

"How Does Language Work?" *Philosophy Now*, May–June, 2012. philosophynow.org/issues/90/How_Does_Language_Work.

"How the Brain Experiences Time." *Neuroscience News*, August 29, 2018. www.neurosciencenews.com/time-perception-9771/.

Ifeanyi, K. C. "This Is Your Brain on Improvisation—and Why Your Creativity Depends on It." *Fast Company*, October 29, 2019. www.fastcompany.com/90421354/this-is-your-brain-on-improvisation-and-why-your-creativity-depends-on-it.

"improvise (v.)." *Online Etymology Dictionary*, www.etymonline.com/search?q=improvise.

Kaiser, David. "Feynman Diagrams." In *Compendium of Quantum Physics*, edited by Daniel Greenberger et al. New York: Springer, 2009, 235–39. SpringerLink. doi:10.1007/978-3-540-70626-7_72.

Kaufman, Sarah L., et al. "Art in an Instant: The Secrets of Improvisation." *Washington Post*, June 7, 2018. www.washingtonpost.com/graphics/2018/lifestyle/science-behind-improv-performance/.

King, Alexander S. "Is Hawking channeling Kant in his explanation of how the arrow of time works?" Philosophy Stack Exchange, April 30, 2015. www.philosophy.stackexchange.com/questions/23408/is-hawking-channeling-kant-in-his-explanation-of-how-the-arrow-of-time-works.

Limb, Charles. Email interview with the author, September 19, 2020.

———. "Your brain on improv." TED: Ideas Worth Spreading, November 2010. www.ted.com/talks/charles_limb_your_brain_on_improv.

Loria, Kevin. "Something Weird Happens to Your Brain When You Start Improvising." Science Alert, May 11, 2016. www.sciencealert.com/something-weird-happens-to-your-brain-when-you-start-improvising.

McPherson, Malinda J., et al. "Emotional Intent Modulates the Neural Substrates of Creativity: An fMRI Study of Emotionally Targeted Improvisation in Jazz Musicians." *Scientific Reports*, 6 (January 2016). PubMed Central. doi:10.1038/srep18460.

Mercer, Michelle. *Footprints: The Life and Work of Wayne Shorter*. New York: Penguin, 2007.

Miller, Jonah. "Reality Is—The Fenyman Path Integral." The Physics Mill, July 16, 2013. www.thephysicsmill.com/2013/07/16/reality-is-the-feynman-path-integral/.

Montagu, Jeremy. "How Music and Instruments Began: A Brief Overview of the Origin and Entire Development of Music, from Its Earliest Stages." *Frontiers in Sociology* 2 (2017): 1–12. doi:10.3389/fsoc.2017.00008.

Montero, Gabriela. "What Choice Do I Have? Gabriela Montero Discusses Classical Improvisation, Composition, and Creative Dissent." The 2019–2020 Kim and Judy Davis Dean's Lecture in the Arts, January 27, 2020, Radcliffe Institute for Advanced Study, Harvard University, Cambridge, Massachusetts.

Moore, Robin. "The Decline of Improvisation in Western Art Music: An Interpretation of Change." *International Review of the Aesthetics and Sociology of Music* 23, no. 1 (1992): 61–84. JSTOR. doi:10.2307/836956.

O'Dowd, Matt. "Feynman's Infinite Quantum Paths." YouTube, uploaded by PBS Space Time, July 7, 2017. www.youtube.com/watch?v=vSFRN-ymfgE.

Pollan, Michael. *How to Change Your Mind: What the New Science of Psychedelics Teaches Us About Consciousness, Dying, Addiction, Depression, and Transcendence.* New York: Penguin, 2018.

Schoenemann, P. Thomas. "Brain Evolution Relevant to Language." In *Language, Evolution, and the Brain,* edited by James W. Minett and William S-Y Wang. Kowloon: City University of Hong Kong Press, 2009, 191–223.

Sherman, Carl. "The Neuroscience of Improvisation." Dana Foundation, June 13, 2011. www.dana.org/article/the-neuroscience-of-improvisation/.

Taruskin, Richard. *The Oxford History of Western Music.* Oxford; New York: Oxford University Press, 2005.

Oxford University Press, 2005. "The Arrow of Time." Episode 11 of *Numb3rs.* Cornell Department of Mathematics. www.pi.math.cornell.edu/~numb3rs/luthy3/thearrowoftime.html.

"The Beginning of Time." Stephen Hawking, https://www.hawking.org.uk/in-words/lectures/the-beginning-of-time.

van Kessel, M. T. M. "The Path-Integral Approach to Spontaneous Symmetry Breaking." arXiv: 0810.1412 [hep-ph], January 7, 2009. Cornell University. arxiv.org/abs/0810.1412.

van Wensem, Casey. "4 Secrets from the World's Best Improvisers That Will Make You a Better Musician." *Soundfly*, April 15, 2016. flypaper.soundfly.com/tips/improvising-secrets-worlds-best-improvisers/.

Weiler, Nicholas. "Brain activity patterns underlying fluent speech revealed." *ScienceDaily*, June 1, 2018. www.sciencedaily.com/releases/2018/06/180601134731.htm.

htm. "What Is the Difference Between Principle of Least Time and Principle of Least Action?" www.quora.com/What-is-the-difference-between-Principle-of-Least-Time-and-Principle-Of-Least-Action.

Wise, Brian, and Naomi Lewin. "Why Don't More Classical Musicians Improvise?" *Conducting Business*, WQXR, January 30, 2015. www.wqxr.org/story/time-return-improvisation-its-classical-roots.

Wright, Lindsay Jordan. "Investigating Improvisation: Music Performance and the Disciplinary Divide." Honors thesis, Wesleyan University, 2010. doi:10.14418/wes01.1.55.

Symmetry Breaking

"About the Suzuki Method." Suzuki Association of the Americas, 1998. suzukiassociation.org/about/suzuki-method/.

Banarjee, Prashant. "CPT symmetry and CP violation. Why energy and momentum are conserved?" YouTube, uploaded by Beyond Sci Fact, January 23, 2019. www.youtube.com/watch?v=j4oSCLZZ2RY.

Barnett, Michael R., and Helen Quinn. "What Is Antimatter?" *Scientific American*, January 24, 2002. www.scientificamerican.com/article/what-is-antimatter-2002-01-24/.

Callender, Craig. "Thermodynamic Asymmetry in Time." In *The Stanford Encyclopedia of Philosophy*, edited by Edward N. Zalta. Metaphysics Research Lab, Stanford University, Winter 2016. www.plato.stanford.edu/archives/win2016/entriesime-thermo/.

Carroll, Sean. "Time-Reversal Violation Is Not the 'Arrow of Time.'" *Sean Carroll: in truth, only atoms and the void*, November 20, 2012. www.preposterousuniverse.com/blog/2012/11/20/time-reversal-violation-is-not-the-arrow-of-time/.

Carter, Christine. "Chinese Mothers Controversy: Why Amy Chua Is Wrong About Parenting." *HuffPost Life*, January 14, 2011. https://www.huffpost.com/entry/chinese-mothers-superior_b_808344.

"Charge, Parity, and Time Reversal (CPT) Symmetry." In *Guide to the Nuclear Wallchart*, ch. 6. www2.lbl.gov/abc/wallchart/chapters/05/2.html.

Choi, Charles Q. "Did Gravity Save the Universe from 'God Particle' Higgs Boson?" *Space.Com*, January 7, 2015. www.space.com/28181-gravity-higgs-boson-universe-destruction.html.

Chua, Amy. "Why Chinese Mothers Are Superior." *Wall Street Journal*, January 8, 2011. www.wsj.com/articles/SB10001424052748704111150457605971352 8698754.

Cooper, Brittney. "Brittney Cooper: How Has Time Been Stolen from People of Color?" *TED Radio Hour*, March 29, 2019. www.npr.org/2019/03/29/707189797/brittney-cooper-how-has-time-been-stolen-from-people-of-color.

"Curtis Institute of Music." *Data USA*, www.datausa.io/profile/university/curtis-institute-of-music.

"Curtis Institute of Music Student Population and Demographics." *College Tuition Compare*, www.collegetuitioncompare.com/edu/211893/curtis-institute-of-music/enrollment/.

"Curtis Institute of Music Student Population and Demographics." *UNIVSTATS*, www.univstats.com/colleges/curtis-institute-of-music/student-population/.

Edelman, Gerald M. *Bright Air, Brilliant Fire: On the Matter of the Mind*. New York: Basic Books, 1992. Internet Archive. archive.org/details/brightairbrillia00gera.

"Galileo's 'falling bodies' experiment re-created at Pisa." *Symmetry Magazine*, October 17, 2009. www.symmetrymagazine.org/breaking/2009/10/17/galileos-falling-bodies-experiment-re-created-at-pisa.

Gnida, Manuel, and Kathryn Jepsen. "Charge-Parity Violation." *Symmetry Magazine*, November 24, 2015. www.symmetrymagazine.org/article/charge-parity-violation.

Gross, David J. "The Role of Symmetry in Fundamental Physics." *Proceedings of the National Academy of Sciences* 93, no. 25 (December 1996): 14256–59. doi:10.1073/pnas.93.25.14256.

Herrero-Valea, Mario. "Nature cares about the direction time flows: T symmetry breaking measured." *Mapping Ignorance*, www.mappingignorance.org/2012/12/20/nature-cares-about-in-which-direction-times-flows-t-symmetry-breaking-measured/.

Hupé, Jean-Michel, and Michel Dojat. "A Critical Review of the Neuroimaging Literature on Synesthesia." *Frontiers in Human Neuroscience* 9 (March 2015). PubMed Central. doi:10.3389/fnhum.2015.00103.

Krause, Beth A. T. "How Domestic Violence Affects Child Custody Colorado." *DivorceNet*, www.divorcenet.com/resources/how-domestic-violence-affects-child-custody-colorado.html.

Lees, J. P., et al. (The BABAR Collaboration). "Observation of Time-Reversal Violation in the B^0 Meson System." *Physical Review Letters* 109, no. 21 (November 2012): 211801. American Physical Society. doi:10.1103/PhysRevLett.109.211801.

Marchese, David. "Yo-Yo Ma and the Meaning of Life." *New York Times Magazine*, November 20, 2020, 13–15.

Nave, C. R. "CPT Invariance." Hyperphysics, Department of Physics and Astronomy, Georgia State University, 2016. www.hyperphysics.phy-astr.gsu.edu/hbase/Particles/cpt.html.

O'Dowd, Matt, and Graeme Gossel. "Our Antimatter, Mirrored, Time-Reversed Universe." YouTube, uploaded by PBS Space Time, January 16, 2019. www.youtube.com/watch?v=L2idut9tkeQ&t=633s.

Oreshkov, Ognyan, and Nicolas J. Cerf. "Operational Formulation of Time Reversal in Quantum Theory." *Nature Physics* 11, no. 10 (October 2015): 853–58. www.nature.com. doi:10.1038/nphys3414.

Paarlberg, Michael Ahn. "Can Asians Save Classical Music?" *Slate Magazine*, February 2, 2012. www.slate.com/culture/2012/02/can-asians-save-classical-music.html.

Palmeri, Thomas, Randolph Blake, and Ren Marois. "What Is Synesthesia?" *Scientific American*, September 11, 2006. www.scientificamerican.com/article/what-is-synesthesia/.

Pitts, Trevor. "Dark Matter, Antimatter, and Time-Symmetry." *arXiv*, March 20, 1999. Cornell University. arxiv.org/html/physics/9812021.

Pössel, Markus. "The Sum Over All Possibilities: The Path Integral Formulation of Quantum Theory." *Einstein Online*, www.einstein-online.info/en/spotlight/path_integrals/.

"Racial/Ethnic and Gender Diversity in the Orchestra Field: A report by the American League of Orchestras with research and data analysis by James Doeser, Ph.D.," *League of American Orchestras*, September 2016. www.ppv.issuelab.org/resources/25840/25840.pdf.

Ramachandran, V. S., and E. M. Hubbard. "Synaesthesia—A Window into Perception, Thought and Language." *Journal of Consciousness Studies* 8, no. 12 (2001): 3–34. web.archive.org/web/20060527085838/http://psy.ucsd.edu/~edhubbard/papers/JCS.pdf.

Science China Press. "Physicists revealed spontaneous T-symmetry breaking and exceptional points in cavity QED." *Phys.Org*, September 13, 2018. phys.org/news/2018-09-physicists-revealed-spontaneous-t-symmetry-exceptional.html.

"Student Population at Curtis Institute of Music." *College Tuition Compare*. https://www.collegetuitioncompare.com/edu/211893/curtis-institute-of-music/enrollment/.

Sutter, Paul. "The Higgs Boson: A Not-So-Godlike Particle." *Space.Com*, May 5, 2017. www.space. com/36724-higgs-boson-not-so-godlike.html.

"symmetry (n.)." *Online Etymology Dictionary*, www. etymonline.com/word/symmetry.

"The Juilliard School Diversity & Student Demographics." *CollegeSimply*, https://www. collegesimply.com/colleges/new-york/the-juilliard-school/students/.

"The Juilliard School Student Population and Demographics." *College Tuition Compare*, www. collegetuitioncompare.com/edu/192110/the-juilliard-school/enrollment/.

"The Juilliard School Student Population and Demographics." *UNIVSTATS*, www.univstats.com/ colleges/the-juilliard-school/student-population/.

Université libre de Bruxelles. "Time-symmetric formulation of quantum theory provides new understanding of causality and free choice." *Phys.org*, phys.org/news/2015-07-time-symmetric-quantum-theory-causality-free.html.

Waldman, Ayelet. "In Defense of the Guilty, Ambivalent, Preoccupied Western Mom." *Wall Street Journal*, January 16, 2011. www.wsj.com/articles/SB10001424 052748703333504576080422577800488.

Wang, Grace. "Interlopers in the Realm of High Culture: 'Music Moms' and the Performance of Asian and Asian American Identities." *American Quarterly* 61, no. 4 (2009): 881–903.

Weyl, Hermann. *Symmetry*. Princeton, NJ: Princeton University Press, 1980.

"What does the term time-translation symmetry mean?" *Reddit*, www.reddit.com/r/askscience/comments/55xhck/what_does_the_term_timetranslation_symmetry_mean/.

Whiteson, Daniel, and Jorge Cham. "This Particle Breaks Time Symmetry." YouTube, uploaded by Veritasium, December 12, 2017. www.youtube.com/watch?v=yArprk0q9eE.

Yoshihara, Mari. *Musicians from a Different Shore: Asians and Asian Americans in Classical Music.* Philadelphia: Temple University Press, 2007.

CHACONNE

Apel, Willi. "Chaconne and Passacaglia." In *The Harvard Dictionary of Music.* 2nd ed. Cambridge: Harvard University Press, 2003, 141 42.

———. "Chaconne." *The Harvard Dictionary of Music.* 4th ed. Cambridge: Harvard University Press, 2003, 155–56.

———. "Rondo." *The Harvard Dictionary of Music.* 4th ed. Cambridge: Harvard University Press, 2003, 741–42.

———. "Sonata da camera, sonata da chiesa." *The Harvard Dictionary of Music.* 2nd ed. Cambridge: Harvard University Press, 1969, 791.

"Bach—Chaconne." *Classic FM*, www.classicfm.com/composers/bach/music/chaconne/.

"Bach's Chaconne: Quotes." *HSU Music*, November 9, 2014. hsumusic.blogspot.com/2014/11/bachs-chaconne-quotes.html.

"Bernard Chazelle—Discovering the Cosmology of Bach." *On Being* podcast with Krista Tippett, November 13, 2014. onbeing.org/programs/bernard-chazelle-discovering-the-cosmology-of-bach/.

Blomster, Wes. "Aspen: Tetzlaff's Bach: Approached with Awe and Affection." *American Record Guide* 64, no. 6 (December 2001): 22–23.

Bragg, Aaron. "Christoph Poppen/The Hilliard Ensemble: *Morimur* (J. S. Bach; Partita in D Minor for Solo Violin BWV 1004; Chorales); ECM New Series." *The Local Planet Weekly* (Spokane, WA), January 24, 2002.

David, Hans T., and Christoph Wolff. *The New Bach Reader: A Life of Johann Sebastian Bach in Letters and Documents.* New York: W. W. Norton, 1999.

Edwards, Robert. "Maria Barbara Bach— Short Biography." *Bach Cantatas Website*, 2007. www.bach-cantatas.com/Lib/Bach-Maria-Barbara.htm.

Eiche, Jon. F., ed. *The Bach Chaconne for Solo Violin: A Collection of Views.* Urbana, IL: American String Teachers Association, 1985.

Eliot, T. S. *Collected Poems 1909–1962.* New York: Harcourt, 1963.

Ford, Trevor. "Is there an underlying symbolic meaning in Bach's D minor Chaconne (violin partita no. 2), if so what?" Quora online forum, June 12, 2016. www.quora.com/Is-there-an-underlying-symbolic-meaning-in-Bachs-D-minor-Chaconne-violin-partita-no-2-if-so-what.

Forkel, Johann Nikolaus. *Johann Sebastian Bach: His Life, Art and Work*. Translated by Charles Sanford Terry. New York: Harcourt, Brace and Howe, 1920. www.gutenberg.org/files/35041/35041-h/35041-h.html.

Helgeson, Mariah. "The Story Behind Bach's Monumental Chaconne." The On Being Project, November 26, 2014. onbeing.org/blog/the-story-behind-bachs-monumental-chaconne/.

Leaver, Robin A. *The Routledge Research Companion to Johann Sebastian Bach*. New York: Routledge, 2016.

Macdonald, Kyle. "Yo-Yo Ma: 'We Live in a Time That Feels Fractured, and Bach Is a Unifying Factor.'" *Classic FM*, September 14, 2018. www.classicfm.com/artists/yo-yo-ma/bach-cello-suites-video/.

Markham, Michael. "The New Mythologies: Deep Bach, Saint Mahler, and the Death Chaconne." *Los Angeles Review of Books*, October 26, 2013. lareviewofbooks.org/article/the-new-mythologies-deep-bach-saint-mahler-and-the-death-chaconne/.

"One Musician Says Bach's Music Has a Special Place in Easter." Daniel Zwerdling interview with Paul Gailbraith. *All Things Considered*, March 27, 2016. www.npr.org/2016/03/27/472067235/one-musician-says-bachs-music-has-a-special-place-in-easter.

Predota, Georg. "Musical Ventriloquism—'Chaconne.'" *Interlude*, March 25, 2013. www.interlude.hk/front/musical-ventriloquismchaconne/.

Smith, Timothy. "Arnstadt (1703–1707)." In *The Canons and Fugues of J. S. Bach*. Flagstaff, Northern Arizona University, 1996. jan.ucc.nau.edu/tas3/arnstadt.html.

———. "Glossary." In *The Canons and Fugues of J. S. Bach*. Flagstaff, Northern Arizona University, 1996. jan.ucc.nau.edu/tas3/glossary.html.

Wight, Colin. "Johann Sebastian Bach (1685–1750)." *British Library*, www.bl.uk/onlinegallery/onlineex/ musicmanu/bach/.

THE STILL POINT OF THE TURNING WORLD

Al-Khalili, Jim, and Johnjoe McFadden. "You're Powered by Quantum Mechanics. No, Really . . ." *The Guardian*, www.theguardian.com/science/2014/ oct/26/youre-powered-by-quantum-mechanics-biology.

"Answering Einstein Decades Later; Quantum Entanglement Is Real." *Science in the News*, November 3, 2015. Graduate School of Arts and Sciences, Harvard University. sitn.hms.harvard.edu/ flash/2015/answering-einstein-decades-later/.

Bell, John Stewart. "Bertlmann's Socks and the Nature of Reality: Invited Address to Meeting of Philosophers and Physicists." CERN. Fondation Hugot du Collège de France, Paris, France, June 17, 1980. cds. cern.ch/record/142461/files/198009299.pdf.

Bennett, Jay. "The Experiment That Blew Open Quantum Mechanics, Explained." *Popular Mechanics*, July 28, 2016. www.popularmechanics.com/science/ a22094/video-explainer-double-slit-experiment/.

Bhatia, Aatish. "The Experiment That Forever Changed How We Think About Reality." *Wired*, January 14, 2014. www.wired.com/2014/01/bells-theorem/.

Brown, Stephen, and Susan Brown. "A Guide to Tango Terminology." Tango Argentino de Tejas, 2000–2014. www.tejastango.com/terminology.html.

Buniy, Roman V., and Stephen D. H. Hsu. "Everything Is Entangled." *Physics Letters B* 718, no. 2 (December 2012): 233–36. ScienceDirect. doi:10.1016/j. physletb.2012.09.047.

Carroll, Larry E. "Lesson Five." *Argentine Tango Dancing,*1997. www.pks.mpg.de/~cug14573/tango/manual/basics_5.html.

"Coincidence." *Online Etymology Dictionary*, www.etymonline.com/word/coincidence.

Cole, K. C. "Wormholes Untangle a Black Hole Paradox." *Quanta Magazine*, April 24, 2015. www.quantamagazine.org/wormhole-entanglement-and-the-firewall-paradox-20150424.

Cooley, Peter. "On Samuel Taylor Coleridge's Biographica Literaria." *Poetry Society of America*, www.poetrysociety.org/psa/poetry/crossroads/old_school/peter_cooley/.

Chu, Jennifer. "Light from Ancient Quasars Helps Confirm Quantum Entanglement." MIT News, August 19, 2018. news.mit.edu/2018/light-ancient-quasars-helps-confirm-quantum-entanglement-0820.

"Delft Scientists Make First 'on Demand' Entanglement Link." TU Delft, June 13, 2018. www.tudelft.nl/en/2018/tu-delft/delft-scientists-make-first-on-demand-entanglement-link/.

"Dr Quantum—Double Slit Experiment." YouTube, uploaded by Brad Cameron, September 13, 2006. www.youtube.com/watch?v=DfPeprQ7oGc.

Eliot, T. S. *Collected Poems 1909–1962*. New York: Harcourt, 1963.

Freedman, Stuart J., and John F. Clauser. "Experimental Test of Local Hidden-Variable Theories." *Physical Review Letters* 28, no. 14 (April 1972): 938–41. doi:10.1103/PhysRevLett.28.938.

Hameroff, Stuart, and Roger Penrose. "Consciousness in the Universe: A Review of the 'Orch OR' Theory." *Physics of Life Reviews* 11, no. 1 (March 2014): 39–78. ScienceDirect. doi:10.1016/j.plrev.2013.08.002.

Joyce, James. *The Dead* [excerpt]. Academy of American Poets. poets.org/poetsorg/poem/dead-excerpt.

"Juan d'Arienzo." *Tangology 101*, October 2, 2010. www.tangology101.com/main.cfm/title/Juan-d'Arienzo/id/62.

Kaiser, David. "How the Hippies Saved Physics: Science, Counterculture, and the Quantum Revival [excerpt]." *Scientific American*, January 30, 2012. www.scientificamerican.com/article/how-the-hippies-saved-physics-science-counterculture-and-quantum-revival-excerpt/.

———. "Is Quantum Entanglement Real?" *New York Times*, December 21, 2017. www.nytimes.com/2014/11/16/opinion/sunday/is-quantum-entanglement-real.html.

Kaku, Michio. "4 Things That Currently Break the Speed of Light Barrier." Big Think, November 9, 2010. bigthink.com/dr-kakus-universe/what-travels-faster-than-the-speed-of-light.

Khutoryansky, Eugene. "Quantum Entanglement, Bell Inequality, EPR paradox." Physics Videos by Eugene Khutoryansky, YouTube, November 7, 2015. www.youtube.com/watch?v=v657Ylwh-_k.

Lenson, David. "The High Imagination." Delivered as the Hess Lecture at the University of Virginia, April 29, 1999, Charlottesville, VA.

Maldacena, Juan, and Leonard Susskind. "Cool Horizons for Entangled Black Holes." *Fortschritte Der Physik* 61, no. 9 (September 2013): 781–811. *arXiv*, July 11, 2013. arxiv.org/abs/1306.0533.

Poltorak, Alexander I. "Covenant Between the Parts as a Metaphor for Quantum Entanglement." *The Times of Israel*, October 18, 2018. blogs.timesofisrael.com/covenant-between-the-parts-as-a-metaphor-for-quantum-entanglement/.

"Professor David Lenson on Life and Teaching." *Massachusetts Daily Collegian*, November 9, 2010. dailycollegian.com/2010/11/professor-david-lenson-on-life-and-teaching/.

"Quantum Entanglement." *ScienceDaily*, www.sciencedaily.com/terms/quantum_entanglement.htm.

"Quantum Entanglement Lab—by Scientific American." Featuring John Matson, George Musser, and Enrique Galvez. *Scientific American*, March 20, 2013. www.youtube.com/watch?v=Z34ugMy1QaA.

"Quantum Mechanics—Are Entangled Photon Particles Really Entangled?" *Physics Stack Exchange*, physics.stackexchange.com/questions/338621/are-entangled-photon-particles-really-entangled.

Robinson, Johnny. "The Heart of Tango." YouTube, performance by Colette Hebert and Richard Council, January 6, 2014. www.youtube.com/watch?v=UqC5ZqRAQuQ&t=8s.

Rovelli, Carlo. *The Order of Time*. New York: Riverhead Books, 2018.

Sorrentino, Fernando. "Apostilles on the 'sad thought that is danced.'" *Letralia, Tierra de Letras,* June 11, 2017. https://letralia.com/articulos-y-reportajes/2017/06/11/apostillas-sobre-el-pensamiento-triste-que-se-baila/&prev=search.

Tate, Karl, et al. "How Quantum Entanglement Works (Infographic)." Live Science, April 8, 2013. www.livescience.com/28550-how-quantum-entanglement-works-infographic.html.

Wisniewski, Thomas. Interview with the author, December 12, 2018.

Woolf, Virginia. *To the Lighthouse.* New York: Harcourt, 1927.

Yeats, William Butler. "Among School Children." *The Collected Poems of W.B. Yeats.* New York: Macmillan, 1989. www.poetryfoundation.org/poems/43293/among-school-children.

CODA: MEMORY IS A HOLOGRAM

Bekenstein, Jacob D. "Information in the Holographic Universe." *Scientific American,* April 1, 2007. doi:10.1038/scientificamerican0407-66sp.

———. "Black Holes and Entropy." *Physical Review D* 7, no. 8, (April 15, 1973): 2333–46. dec1.sinp.msu.ru/~panov/Lib/Papers/GR/Bekenstein1973Entropy.pdf.

"Black Holes." *NASA Science,* science.nasa.gov/astrophysics/focus-areas/black-holes.

Goodman, Lawrence. "The universe is a hologram and other mind-blowing theories in theoretical physics." phys.org, March 6, 2018. phys.org/news/2018-03-universe-hologram-mind-blowing-theories-theoretical.html.

Hawking, Stephen, and Leonard Mlodinow, "The Elusive Theory of Everything." *Scientific American*, October 1, 2010. www.scientificamerican.com/article/the-elusive-thoery-of-everything/.

Hooft, Gerard 't. "Dimensional Reduction in Quantum Gravity." *arXiv*, March 20, 2009. Cornell University. arxiv.org/abs/gr-qc/9310026.

———. "The Holographic Principle."*arXiv*, May 16, 2000. Cornell University. arxiv.org/abs/hep-th/0003004.

Maldacena, Juan M. "The Large N Limit of Superconformal Field Theories and Supergravity." *arXiv*, January 22, 1998. Cornell University. arxiv.org/abs/hep-th/9711200.

O'Dowd, Matt. "The Holographic Universe Explained." YouTube, uploaded by PBS Space Time, April 10, 2019. www.youtube.com/watch?v=klpDHn8viX8.

Stromberg, Joseph. "Some Physicists Believe We're Living in a Giant Hologram — and It's Not That Far-Fetched." Vox, June 29, 2015. www.vox.com/2015/6/29/8847863/holographic-principle-universe-theory-physics.

Susskind, L. "The World as a Hologram." *arXiv*, September 28, 1994. Cornell University. arxiv.org/abs/hep-th/9409089.

Timmer, John. "How a Holographic Universe Emerged from Fight With Stephen Hawking." *Wired*, August 1, 2011. www.wired.com/2011/08/hawking-holographic-universe/.

Trosper, Jaime. "The Holographic Universe Principle." *Futurism*, December 12, 2013. futurism.com/the-holographc-universe-principle-what-is-what-should-never-be.

Wolchover, Natalie. "How Our Universe Could Emerge
as a Hologram." *Quanta Magazine*, February 21,
2019. www.quantamagazine.org/how-our-universe-
could-emerge-as-a-hologram-20190221/.

Wood, Charlie. "What is Quantum Gravity?" Space.
com, August 27, 2019. www.space.com/quantum-
gravity.html.

Bellevue Literary Press is devoted to publishing literary fiction and nonfiction at the intersection of the arts and sciences because we believe that science and the humanities are natural companions for understanding the human experience. We feature exceptional literature that explores the nature of consciousness, embodiment, and the underpinnings of the social contract. With each book we publish, our goal is to foster a rich, interdisciplinary dialogue that will forge new tools for thinking and engaging with the world.

To support our press and its mission, and for our full catalogue of published titles, please visit us at blpress.org.

BELLEVUE LITERARY PRESS
New York

CPSIA information can be obtained
at www.ICGtesting.com
Printed in the USA
JSHW051226030622
26500JS00006B/6